Mothers & Daughters Anthology II

Contents

Foreword	iv
Penny for Your Thoughts	5
Carolyn Lumpkin	29
I Got You, Too	34
Kim Clarkson-Elliott	45
Just Breathe	51
Shandrika Milligan	65
Longing to Belong	69
Sabrina R. Owens	95
Rusty's Restoration	100
Annette Beggarly	139
Epilogue	141
Healing Declarations, Prayer & Scriptures	145

Mothers & Daughters Anthology II

Foreword

We all know parenting does not come with a manual. If it did, how accurate would it really be? There is so much to know and learn about your children, it would be impossible to put it all in a book. Especially since no two children are alike and are as different as two mismatched socks even if they are born of the same parents. How do I know this? I am living it. As a mother has an impeccable gift of recognizing early on the stark difference in the personality of their children. Imagine how well equipped she must be to identify from her child's crying what they need. How does she know a hunger cry from a wet diaper cry from an I am not feeling well cry? Oh, to be a mother is not for the faint at heart. If you are not impressed by a mother's ability to read the notes of a cry as if she was reading sheet music, you must be in awe of how she can identify her child's call for mom even in a crowd. Even as a mother myself, I find that pretty impressive. Perhaps it's the connection that starts in utero that passes its bond through eternity. This bond is a reflection of 1 Corinthians 13:4-7 as "love is patient, love is kind; love does not envy or boast; it is not proud. It does not dishonor others, it is not self-seeking, it is not easily angered, it keeps no record of wrongs. Love does not delight in evil but rejoices with the truth. Love bears all things, believes all things, hopes all things, endures all things."

It's important for a mother and daughter to see each other, not for what they desire each to be, but for who God has purposed each to be. When we realize this, we are able to create a relationship that transcends all circumstances whether we are standing apart or together. I considered that when a mother is pregnant with a daughter, she is carrying two generations. How? A female fetus develops all the eggs she will ever have while in the mother's womb. Wow, what an amazing realization of how important a mother and daughter's relationship is to future generations. Whatever a mother carries, whether it be joy or depression, peace or chaos, respect for oneself and others or disrespect, hope or discouragement, love or hate, faith, or fear, she passes it on to her daughter. But even still, she, they, stand in the midst of it all as "Wounded Healers" as I mentioned in the first anthology. (Should I explain this theory again?) (If so, here it is.)

"The Wounded Healer Theory" by Marion Conti-O'Hare addresses the effective or ineffective coping strategies after exposure or experiencing personal trauma. It explains that if trauma is dealt with effectively, the pain is consciously recognized, transformed, and transcended into healing. This process ultimately leads to healing, despite the remaining scars.

As you delve into the pages of *Mothers & Daughters: Their Story, Their Way, Only They Can Tell It, Anthology II*, may you become emerged in the stories of these five women and become inspired by their journeys. For as they are equipped for the journey as a "Wounded Healer," so are you!

Jacqueline Pitt

Mothers & Daughters Anthology II

Mothers & Daughters Anthology II

Dedication

To Pennie, who is a fighter and an overcomer, and to Jesus, Who is the source of her power. And to all of my family, church family and others who prayed so powerfully while she was at UVA. Jesus heard our prayers.

Mothers & Daughters Anthology II

Penny for Your Thoughts

By Carolyn Lumpkin

Tuesday morning, very early before the sun rose the week of Thanksgiving in 2018, my granddaughter woke me up and told me that her mama was talking backwards, or something was wrong with her. They have lived with me, and a grandson as well, for a few years. So I got up and went in her bedroom and saw my 48-year-old daughter. I knew she had a tooth infection because her jaw was swollen really big. Being awakened out of a dead sleep, I said, "Give me just a minute to get myself awake, and we will take her to the emergency room."

In a few minutes, my granddaughter came back in and said, "Mom has gotten worse." We called the ambulance. Pennie was able to walk down the steps, and when she got to the emergency room, she was delirious. She didn't understand why the workers were doing what they were doing to her. So they intubated her in order to treat her. She was scheduled to have her teeth all taken out the week before. When she went, she had a cold or sinus infection starting, so that oral surgeon did not remove her teeth.

That was the beginning of my daughter Pennie Dawn's journey. In our town, we did not have an eye doctor that came to the hospital. The infection had rapidly moved up to her eye, as it was very swollen. As a result, she was kept in ICU but transferred to UVA in Charlottesville the next day.

On Thanksgiving Day, Pennie had two surgeries. The doctors removed all her teeth since they did not know which one the infection was coming from. She was scheduled to have all of them removed anyway. Then the ear, nose and throat doctor scraped out all the infection they could from her sinuses, but at that point they realized it had already gone to her brain. And at some point she had strokes. Every test they did showed so much brain damage and so much infection that they didn't think that she would make it.

My other daughter and Pennie's daughter stayed in Charlottesville for one month with her. My daughter rarely left the hospital, except when I would make her go to the hotel to sleep. I went to the hotel most nights with my granddaughter to try and get a little rest. Pennie's other daughter, her son, my three sisters and others made several trips from Danville where we live to Charlottesville during that month.

The doctors were very negative. They said there was too much brain damage from so much infection and the strokes. She would be a vegetable. If she lived, she wouldn't walk, talk or any of the things that give you any quality of life.

During the month that we were there, we had many family meetings in the room down the hall to disconnect everything from her and let her pass. The doctors finally got me to agree to disconnect all of the tubes that went in her in many locations and the respirator. I did not want to do that. I didn't think that we had given God enough time to work.

Also during this time, we had multiple prayer chains going on back home at several churches, including my own church, and within our friends, and families. With every family meeting, I kept telling them we had not given God enough time to work. The medical team kept telling me the damage was too severe. Pennie could not survive and to do the humane thing and let her just die peacefully. I did not think I could bury a child. We begged God to heal her and spare her life.

The doctors continued to be negative. Several would get very close to my face and say, "I don't think you know what we are trying to tell you, Mrs. Lumpkin. Your daughter cannot make it. The severe infection and the damage from the strokes… you just do not understand. She cannot live."

I would sit in the chair and think, "But you don't understand that my God is more able than any doctor's medicine."

When I finally agreed to have everything disconnected, all her children, my sisters, my pastor, his wife, another pastor of a friend, and several people came to pray one last time. I said, "God gave me a word some years back. And giving up I didn't think was right and did not line up with the word that I received from the Lord a few years ago." My pastor said that sometimes he thinks that maybe we think we hear from God, but don't. I can't remember exactly how he put it. But even he thought at this point we needed to just disconnect and let her go.

That night, they disconnected everything. I sent all my family to the hotel. I stayed all night by myself. I brought her into this world, and I was going to stay to see her leave this world by myself. Two of her children were teenagers and the oldest one was a young adult and pregnant with her second child. I just didn't think they ought to be there at the end of Pennie's life.

After all of the disconnections, Pennie did not pass away. She breathed on her on. More tests were conducted that showed more infection, and Pennie was going to be sent home on hospice. This was the week before Christmas. Certainly, this was not what I wanted to do. I wanted to stay at the hospital and have more IV antibiotics and other treatments, but the medical team said they needed to send her home because strokes did so much damage to her brain. Following a month of strong, strong antibiotics, she was worse, not better.

The night before she was to leave the hospital, I got up and crossed the room.

Pennie opened her eyes and her eyes followed me the rest of the night. She even tried to talk. We arrived home after the very long ride from Charlottesville back to Danville. The home health agency set up equipment for us, and hospice care was sent in the next day to help us. She began to swallow and tried to talk again.

When we gave Pennie a pen and paper, she wrote. So, we knew her brain was not dead. Although badly damaged, it still was working. She knew us all. She knew what to do with everything you put in her hand. I knew with more prayer she would come back to us fully. I truly believed that God had given us a Christmas miracle.

After Christmas, Pennie was reevaluated at our local emergency room and sent to Duke hospital, where she stayed for one month with more IV antibiotic therapies and other treatments. She talked a little and wrote a lot when she had pen and paper. She seemed to be coming back to us. Due to insurance, she had to leave Duke and go to Virginia Baptist in Lynchburg, where she stayed another month.

Mid-February, the week of her 49th birthday, Pennie had a massive grand mall seizure for an hour and a half that set her back drastically. She had not had any seizures at all and no more strokes since the beginning of her journey at that point. We were back at square one. But she stayed there for a month and then was sent to a rehab center in Martinsville about 30 minutes from my home. Due to no rooms being available locally, after being there a month, we finally got her in a local rehab in our town where she remains to this day.

We have seen God raise Pennie up almost from the dead. God was so faithful to breathe new life back into her when all the doctors said there was no hope. I think there is always hope, until the last breath is drawn. It was really unreal how many people prayed for her, including pastors that I had met over the years. Whole congregations were praying. Some called me daily to pray. I can't remember everything that happened during that time. My sister set up a Facebook page, entitled Pennie Dawn Edward's Journey- Tracking God's Amazing Love, to inform everyone of her progress and track God's goodness. Most of her story is there.

    I just know that God was very faithful to see me through this awful time and gave me the strength to help take care of her. He's still taking care of her and me, and the peace that He gave me after this began still resides in me, although we had our times of battling insurance, no room at rehabs, and other events.

One of the pastors from my town that I had met years ago mailed us a healing CD that she had made. We played it all night and played praise music and hymns when the healing CD wasn't playing. We stood on God's Word, and we saw a miracle unfold before our eyes. Pennie woke up and could see, began to talk, eat, even move around in her bed. She always called me Mama when I went in her room and always called her daughters Baby, which is what she called them before her illness.

Pennie always tried to tell us something. Sometimes the words were very clear. Sometimes they were not clear at all. But she clearly talks to us with her eyes, and we felt she was coming all the way back for a total healing when the shutdown happened at the nursing home due to COVID. Now that we are able to visit again, we are kind of starting all over. While the shutdown of the nursing home kept all of our family away, it shut her down also. She doesn't talk, but on God's Word and His promises that she will be healed. Maybe not like we would like it to be.... But........ whatever God gives us, we will take....

Watching the transition of having no hope, to watching Pennie feed herself, interact with those who visited, the words she spoke and the smile we could see in her eyes told all the family and nurses that Pennie was on her way to victory in healing. COVID came as a curse to everyone that was in hospitals and nursing homes when everything shut down. Did anyone realize the detriment that would occur when you go almost two years without family visiting and interaction with those you love? Can anyone imagine what Pennie or anyone in such circumstances thought in their minds? All the progress family had witnessed in Pennie Dawn was as though someone came in and wiped that board clean. She no longer fed herself, no longer interacted with anyone and starred into space as if she really didn't see us. Maybe she was so hurt and could not express herself? We just don't know what she thought. COVID killed more than those following the vaccine mandates. It killed the spirit that lives in us all who are encouraged by touch, hugs, and interaction.

    This struggle has been so real and so very time consuming, trying to get Pennie therapies that she needs. When a person like Pennie is dependent on government assisted help, Medicaid is all that is supplied in a nursing home facility. There is no funding for anything except having meals prepared and delivered, since she can no longer feed herself. Nurses don't have time to feed her because it takes at least an hour to be sure she is properly fed. Her weight continues to drop even though there are ladies I hired and pay to come in three times a day. There are clinics in the USA that would take her and give her physical therapy, speech therapy and more, but the cost is astronomical. With so many helpmates in the world that would assist Pennie immensely, why isn't there help to bring her back fully without such costs? Government funded programs are not for the benefit of health and healing. They are merely there to keep you alive and not well.

In the very beginning, I asked one of the agents at her insurance company, wouldn't it make much better sense to give people intense rehab for the first six months to a year? They could get well, go home and be taken care of by their family, if not by themselves, versus just giving them food, personal care, and no therapy, keeping them alive for the next 30 to 40 years with dependent care. The agent agreed with me, but Pennie's insurance does not cover anything but basic care still. Any extra rehab or helping her to eat is coming from me.

It is our prayer that one day this will change, and somehow through God's grace and mercy such a program will be available to Pennie, to not only bring her back to health but back 100% for her children, grandchildren and especially to me, her mom.

We give God the glory. He is the great physician, and we WILL see this happen in HIS time. Please pray with us and come in agreement with us. I still pray daily, Psalms 91, as I did all those months she was in the hospital.

Pennie and her son Stuart, daughter Angelica, and daughter Christina. Picture was made almost a year to the day Pennie became sick. They are now 25, 26 and 31, and Pennie is 53 years old. Hope you have a great day!

Mothers & Daughters Anthology II

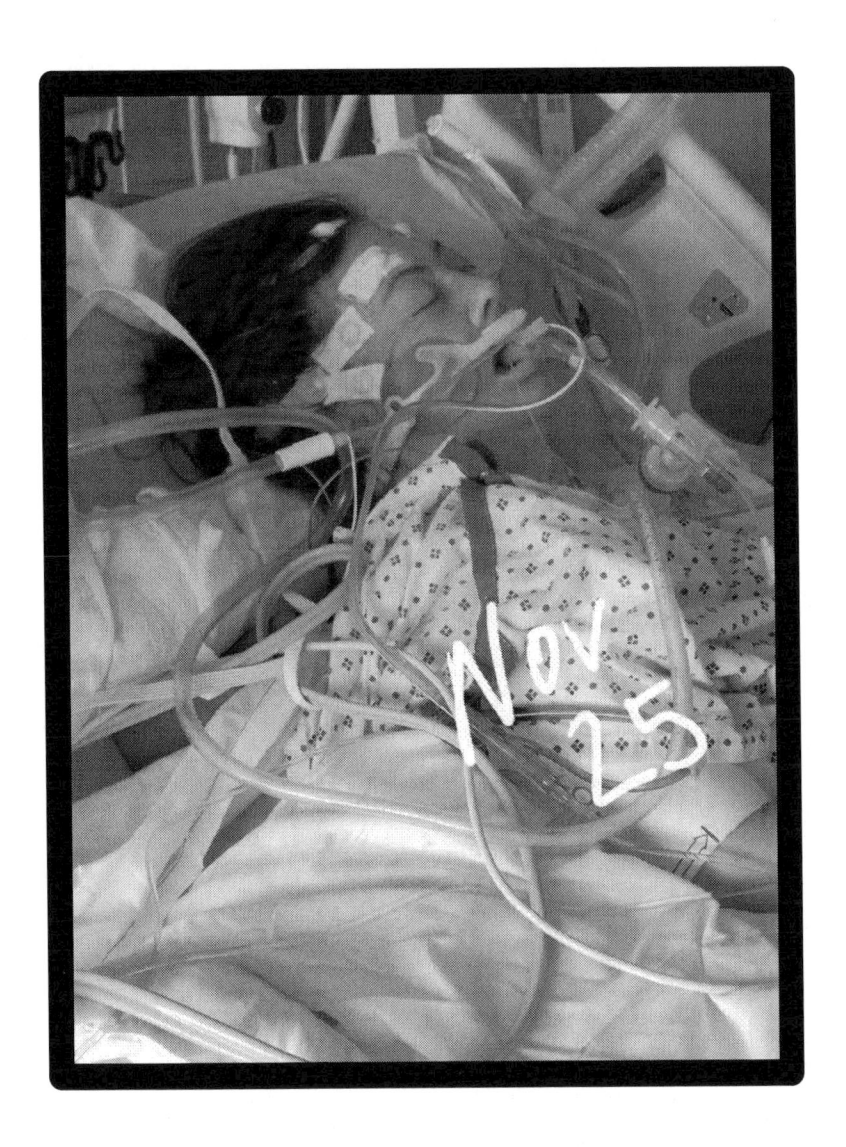

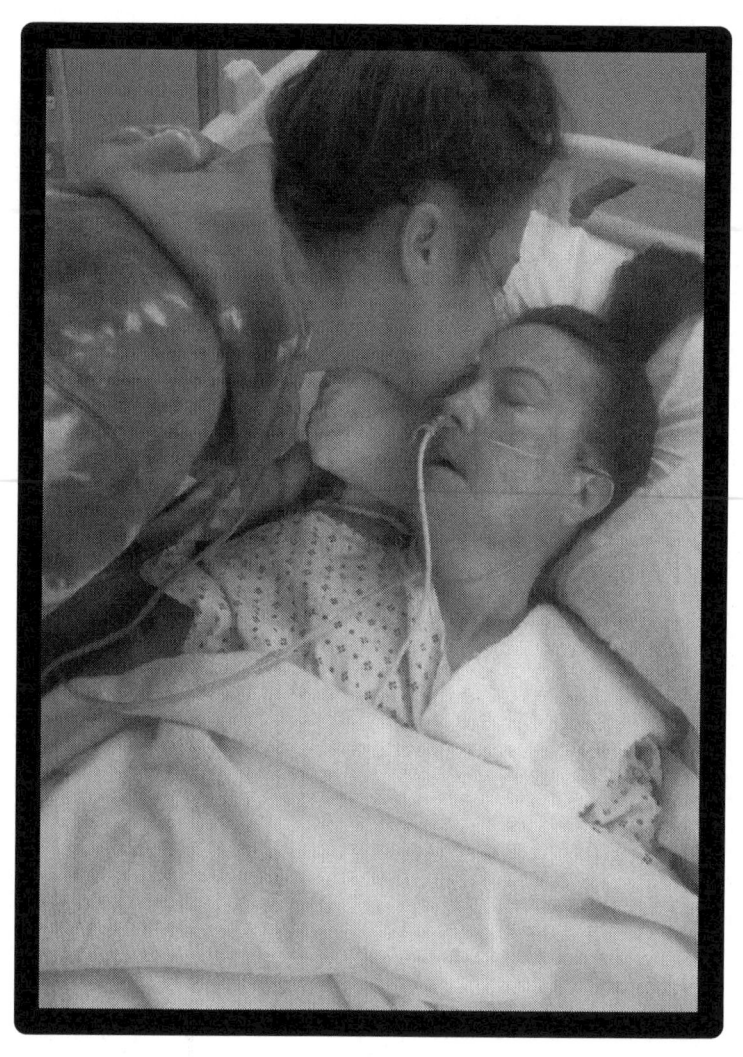

Pennies' daughter Angelica stayed by her side almost the entire month we were at UVA. This picture was after many of the breathing devices were removed.

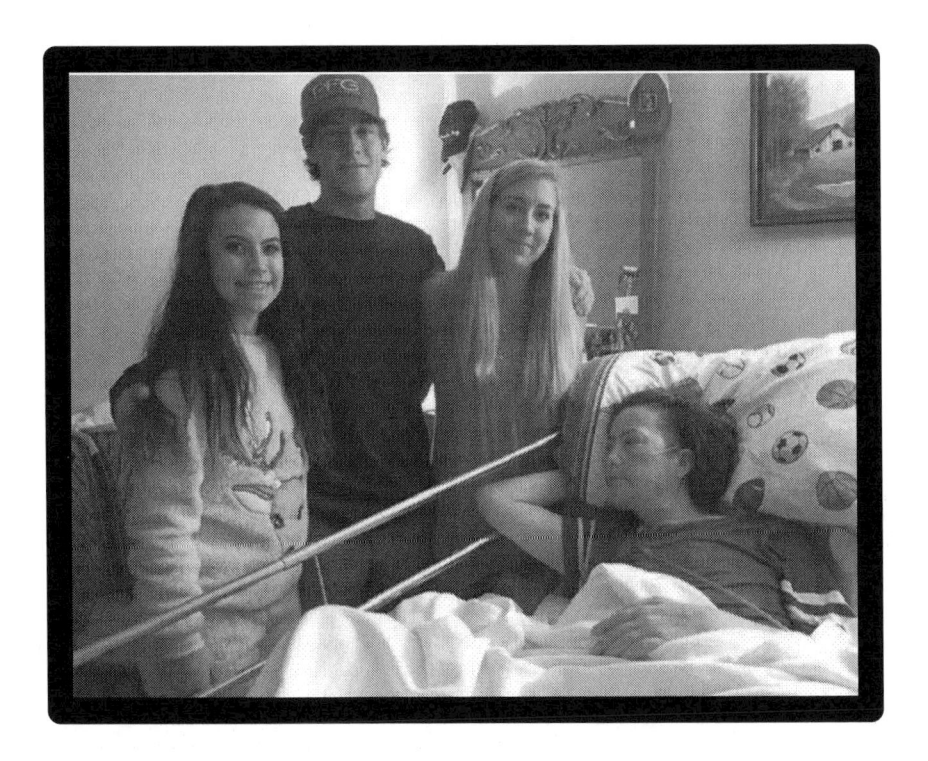

After a month at UVA, Pennie was sent home on hospice to die. She came out of the coma just a few days before she was released from the hospital. At Christmas, she talked to everyone. This is her three children at our home on Christmas.

Mothers & Daughters Anthology II

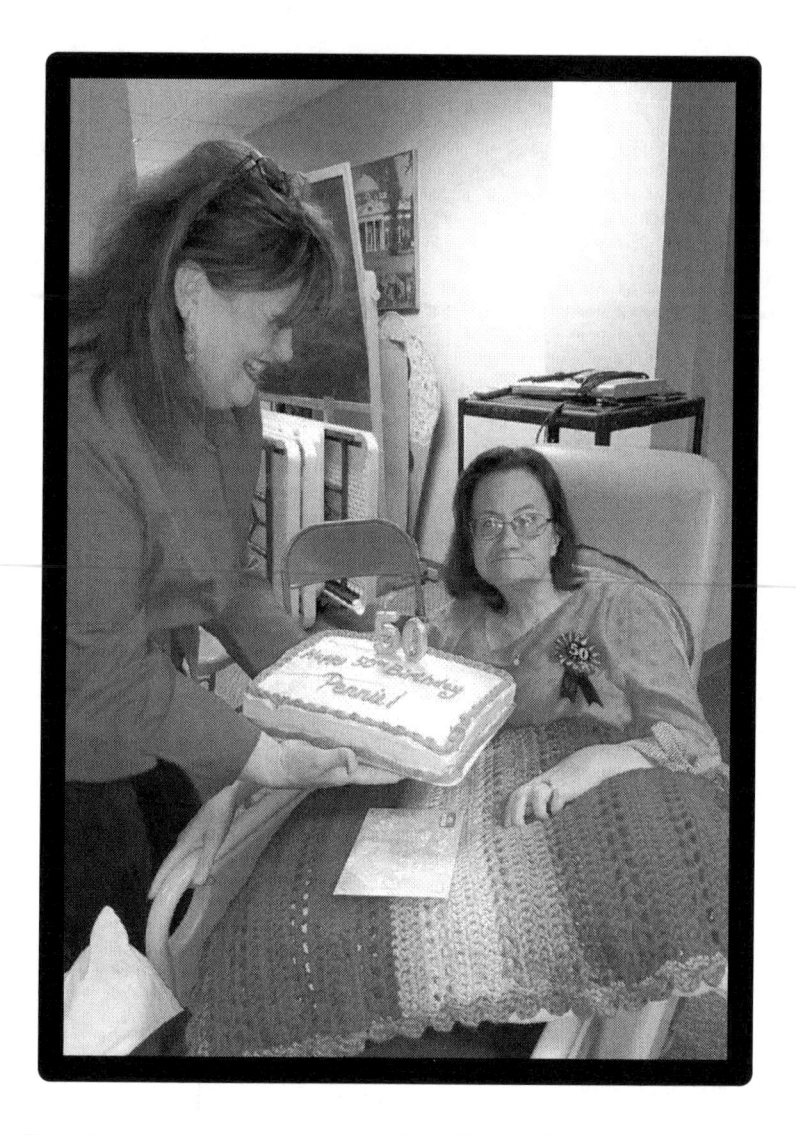

Pennie and my sister, her aunt, at Pennie's 50th birthday party

Pennie and her son at her 50th birthday party that the doctors at UVA said she would not see. She did see it and she enjoyed it very much. She knew it was her birthday.

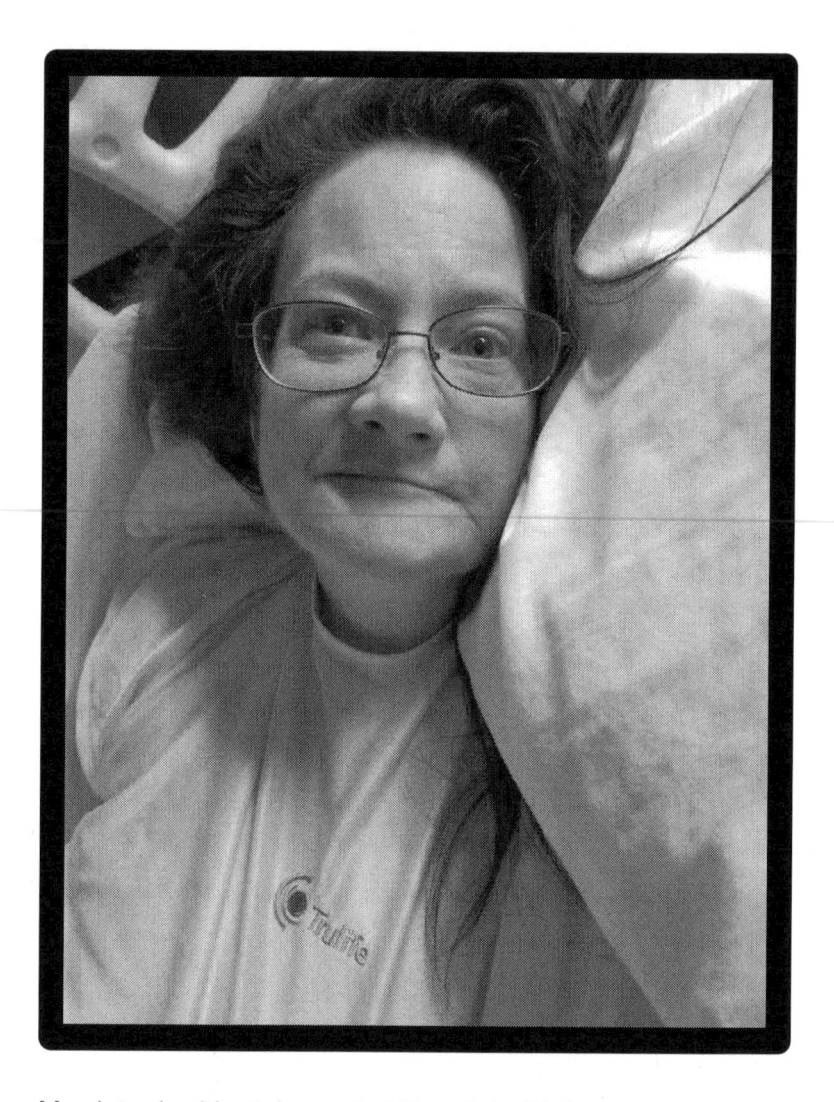

My sister had just decorated Pennie's Christmas (2019) tree at the rehab, and Pennie was talking to her with her eyes.

Mothers & Daughters Anthology II

Pennie is a grandmother again. This was at her 53rd birthday party in February with her son Stuart, Emily and three-month-old Declan.

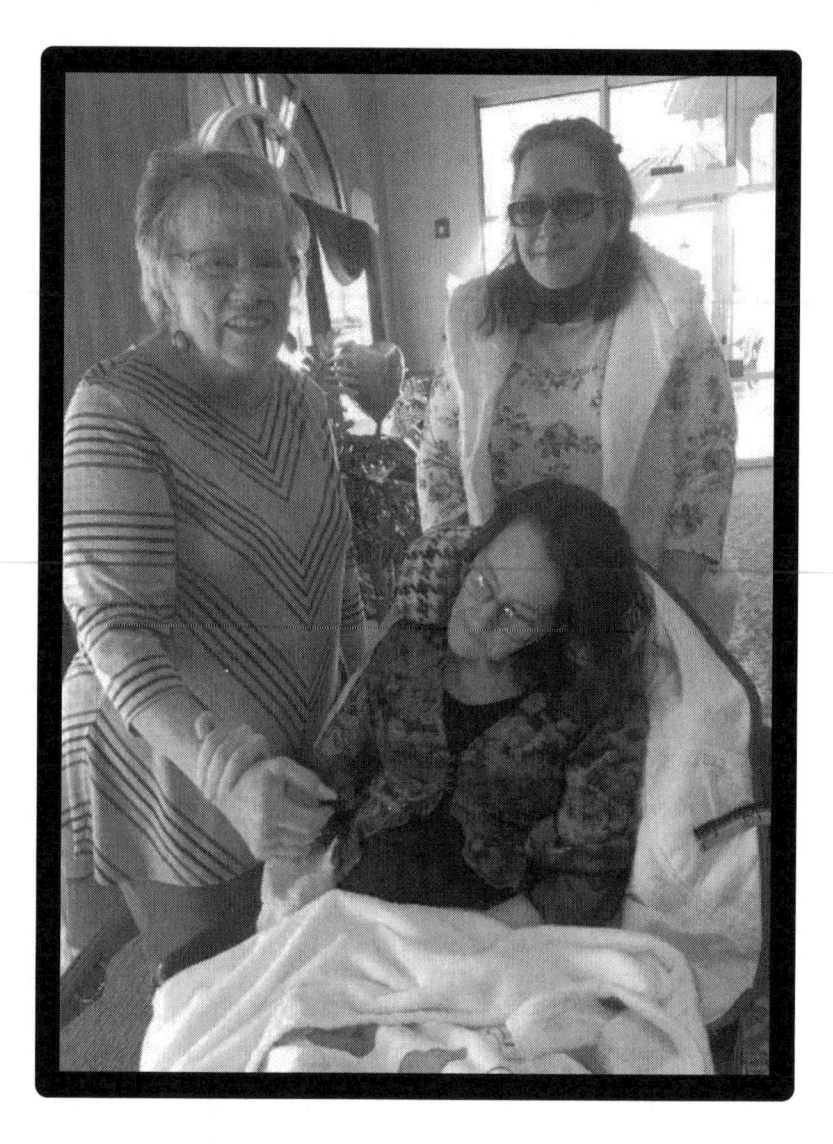

Pennie, her sister Angie, and me. This represents the unfailing love of a mother who refused to give up on her daughter even when doctors said, "No." God said, "YES.

Mothers & Daughters Anthology II

About the Author

Carolyn Lumpkin

Carolyn Lumpkin grew up just outside of the city limits in Pittsylvania County, Virginia and her daddy was a tobacco farmer. She worked either in the garden or in the tobacco fields. It was a hard life, but Carol's mother always said it was the best life one could have.

In 1947, Carolyn graduated from high school and got married in 1965. In 2005, her husband of 40 years passed away from cancer after treatments and a battle of about two years. They have two daughters and a son, nine grandchildren and seven great grandchildren with another due in August. When this family gathers, it is a house full of love, noise, laughter, and chatter.

After many years of bookkeeping and managing offices, Carolyn opened The Bra Lady Boutique in 1999. The store celebrates its 24th year in May 2023. Carolyn says, "It's really been my ministry because of the close connection that you get with all of your customers. In this last year or so, I have sort of semi-retired, but I am still a vital part of everything that goes on in the business. It's hard to retire totally from something that you love. We do custom fitted bras for ladies and also have mastectomy products for ladies who have survived breast cancer and other breast surgeries."

Carolyn's oldest daughter from her story "Penny for Your Thoughts" remains in a local rehab, and the family continues to fight for all the things that she needs to give her quality of life following the strokes and the major setbacks from the shutdown of the rehab facility during the COVID outbreaks.

Dedication

To my mom Betty Lindsey Clarkson. Her spirit and her love of writing letters and notes have encouraged me through my journey. And to my Aunt Thrisha Ann Shiver for her love and support in my journey.

I Got You, Too

By Kim Clarkson-Elliott

Born in Columbia, South Carolina, the youngest of three children, I was the daughter of a beautiful woman, a sharp dresser and classy lady with the attitude to match. My father was a laid-back man that always greets people with a smile. I asked my mother why she, being a neat freak, hooked up with a man that wore a tee shirt as a shirt. My mother said, "Marry your opposite so your relationship will not be boring." However, in the end it became too much entertainment, and they divorced when I was in third grade.

After their divorce my mother moved back to her hometown Union, SC with my two brothers and me. My mother and my maternal grandmother were the two women who always made sure I was happy and able to experience all the opportunities I wanted to participate in. They always told me to be myself and to not just be beautiful on the outside, but on the inside also to learn from your mistakes and never be afraid to ask for help, because people can only say "yes" or "no."

My grandmother and I share the same middle name "Elizabeth." My grandmother owned a restaurant up until I went off to college. I helped run the kiddie dances on Saturdays and helped out in the restaurant during the week. Those were some of the best memories. I never knew how amazing and smart my grandmother was until she sent me a card in college. I still have it; she signed with an X. I knew right then I could do anything in life if I set my mind to it. In college, I started out majoring in psychology, but my love for art caused me at the end of my freshman year to change to art with my mother's approval. But not at first. She said I needed something to fall back on and make a decent living. Four years before I became an art teacher, the two people who inspired me to be myself and stated that life is what you make it died within six months of each other. My support system was gone. My mother, who advised me on issues that I couldn't see, who supported me in good and bad situations, said that I could do anything I set my mind to, and to not give up on myself or the things that are most important to me, was gone suddenly.

I think my strong foundation and childhood experience with my brothers helped me make it so far through the second chapter in my life. I met my husband early in my adult life and had two beautiful children. My son was my first born; he was a happy baby who smiled all of the time. He was very playful, loved a football and hot rod cars and never asked for something to eat. The first time, at the age of three, he asked for Chinese food one day after his father and I picked him up from day care. Right then his father said, "Did you hear that? We are going to get some right now."

Around the time my son was six and my daughter was four, I started to notice some differences in the two. One day, I visited my son's class and noticed that he was sitting at a table away from other students. The teacher stated his social skills with the other students interfered with student learning. I was not notified, and I felt heartbroken for my son. I asked for him to be moved to another class.

In fourth grade, my son was saying mean things to students under his breath as they were walking past him in class. When the behavior referrals started to come more often, my son cried and his eyes would look as though someone else other than him had done it. My son's grades started to fall, and the teacher said my son wasn't very focused in class and was not keeping up in his schoolwork. The school had my son tested, and this resulted in an IEP offering services to help my son to be more successful in school.

Being pulled out for extra help did help with my son's grades and class work during fourth and fifth grades. Shortly after, I started to notice signs of frustration from him with other students at his school. My son also started showing anger toward other students in class again. His pediatrician referred us to a child psychologist who diagnosed my son with ODD and ADHD. For the ADHD, the doctor tried a stimulant medication. Over a period of time, this medication made my son more aggressive and very moody. Then a nonstimulant was prescribed where I saw no differences. We continued to reason with my son over bad choices he continued to make.

In the sixth grade, my son became more defensive and started getting in our face. Right then, we knew we needed another medication. This caused me to admit him to the children's ward at the hospital. There my son stayed for fourteen days to find a medication or see if there was another diagnosis to describe his behavior. He was released on a medication to slow his reaction to situations and one to help him sleep better. This medication was working but seemed to not show any effectiveness when he was faced with difficult situations where he had to give his opinion or be asked to do something he didn't want to do.

My son started eighth grade and started to not listen again. He was acting as if he wasn't on medication and was remitted to the children's hospital where they recommended my son be put in a smaller setting. We enrolled my son into private schools, one was military and one alternative school. My son was kicked out of both private schools and completed the alternative wilderness program. He was returned to public school the beginning year of high school. I could see that he was trying to have friends but was easily influenced by lack of focus in his studies and peer pressure, as well as the inability to make good decisions.

To get back and forth from school, at first my son was riding in the front of the bus with no problem. But his wrong decisions at the back of the bus caused him to be kicked off the bus. A taxi had to be provided to take him back and forth to school, When we would arrive home, he would be gone and no homework was completed. Then we ended up paying for my son to go to an afterschool program to complete his schoolwork. He would jump out of the taxi and run five miles home.

I truly knew one morning that I had to get my son the right help when he came in the door of the kitchen and said, "You can't save me." I turned to him and said, "I will die trying," and he walked away.

I wondered who else in my family may have heard voices. I wondered some days was it my mother? I wish I had the opportunity to hear her journey in her own words and not just my interpretation. As time passed with mental health counseling, some days were good. But some days my son became aggressive. He would try to confront me when I said he couldn't go with his friends or walk out the neighborhood. The police were called on many occasions, and he was being referred to the mental health counselor at school. Even with medication, nothing was working. We felt we had tried everything to get my son on track. It felt as if we were going around and around in circles. It was as if we were living in with someone other than the son we knew some years ago.

Then one day, we refused to let my son go hang out with his friends, and the comments back and forth with us were the worst I had observed. The police were called and my son was admitted back to the hospital. He was there two days, and no medication was changed, and no resources were provided on next steps. On the third day, I refused to pick my baby up from the same hospital. I had him at sixteen years ago. That evening, my daughter asked me if I was going to pick her brother up. I turned my head and said, "I got you and your brother, too."

Tired and feeling like I had failed at motherhood, I remembered that I had asked the Lord for a beautiful brown baby girl the same color as my mother. And my first child to be a boy. I love them so much. No words can describe how I felt when he came in the world. I am here for him, no matter what good or bad. I Got You, Too!

My son's journey is ongoing. My prayer for my son is that one day he will be able to write his own chapter. He has the best support group ever, a praying grandfather and grandmother, two awesome aunts, one that tells me every day that she finally sees and believes me. Both aunts pray for my son every day. I am sorry it took so long to see that no one is perfect and to respect others for who they are. We must help others when they are not mentally able to help themselves.

Mothers & Daughters Anthology II

About the Author

Kim Elizabeth Clarkson-Elliott

Kim Elizabeth Clarkson-Elliott was born in Hopkins, South Carolina. However, she grew up and spent most of her childhood in Union, South Carolina among a great support system including her mother, aunts, uncle, grandparents, and other close relatives. Kim was always a very creative child and excelled in art at a very young age. She competed in and consistently won art competitions during her school years. As a high school student, she was selected to attend the prestigious South Carolina's Governor's School of the Arts and Humanities for academically and artistically gifted students. While there, she shared her talent with others and represented Union High School at the state level.

Kim attended South Carolina State University and completed a degree in Visual Art. She later continued her education and completed her master's degree in educational counseling with a focus on middle grades. Kim is an awesome art teacher in Richland School District One. She has been teaching for over 20 years and thoroughly enjoys being a beacon of artistic light for her students. She is also an innovative entrepreneur. Kim's passion is healing through art, which inspired her to create and develop a company called Paint Therapy Express. Through research and educational experiences, she found that art therapy combined with mental therapies can be used with individuals, couples, or groups to reshape brains and alter thoughts in a more positive, balanced way.

Kim and her husband Reginald currently reside in the Columbia, South Carolina area with their two wonderful children, Chase and Chandler. Kim hopes that her story, "I Got You, Too," can inspire and encourage others.

One of her favorite sayings is "Life is what you make it."

Mothers & Daughters Anthology II

Mothers & Daughters Anthology II

Dedication

For my children

Everything I do is with you in mind.

Just Breathe

By Shandrika Milligan

Where am I? How did I get here? Wait. Why can't I move? Why am I laying on this table, unable to speak or move? Why are people looking at me? Are they drugging me? I just feel so tired.

Two weeks earlier...

On the first day back to work after summer break, Friday, August 13, 2021, I go in to complete packets for the upcoming school year. I talk and eat with friends and then head home. Early Sunday morning, I have a runny nose and a slight headache, nothing my usual sinus medicine can't fix right? Monday comes in and I feel horrible, my head is pounding. I have intolerable congestion, and I am super tired. I immediately called my doctor's office for a same day appointment for my usual Solumedrol to combat this sinus infection I probably have. I head to my 10 AM appointment after dropping my mom off for her total knee replacement surgery. At 10:30, I was diagnosed with COVID. I think "there is no way I can have COVID. I've been to Miami, Vegas, Houston, Puerto Rico, and Charlotte this year celebrating turning 40 with no issues."

But August 16th changed my life in a way I never thought it could. The first two days were bearable. It mostly consisted of headaches and body aches. I thought, "If this is all it is, then I'll be okay." Days four and five brought the absence of smell and taste, but days five through ten were the worst. I vomited every day, multiple times a day. I couldn't even keep water down, so I sucked on ice chips.

My kids were troopers. They went between my mom, who was recovering from surgery, to me suffering with COVID. My daughter, who was a freshman at Benedict at the time, attended to me while my son, who was working, would attend to my mom. They had their rotation down pack. My youngest, who was just starting face to face classes, was managing as well. Because they were doing so much, I tried to do as much as I could for myself. My body was so weak that I could only take five-minute showers and then literally crawl back to bed after laying on the floor to gather energy. It became unbearable, so I called my best friend's cousin, who happens to be a nurse practitioner, for advice. She came over, dressed in full PPE to administer fluids. That lasted a full day, but the vomiting began again. She then instructed me to go to MedCare, where they could possibly give a COVID medication. I stayed in MedCare for 10 minutes before an ambulance was called due to my deteriorating condition. As the paramedics worked on me in the ambulance, I could see my daughter crying, not knowing what was going on the inside with me. I was too weak to cry along with her. Once in the ER, I was diagnosed with COVID Pneumonia and placed on oxygen. There were no visitors allowed due to the pandemic, so we communicated through texting. I was admitted, but things SEEMED to be looking up. But unbeknownst to me, I was still critical.

I don't remember when the talk began about being put on a ventilator. But later, I knew the conversation existed, because I reread texts and I was telling my friend, the nurse practitioner, I was scared and asked if she could talk to my kids. She and my daughter were the two contacts on my paperwork when I was admitted.

On Monday, August 30, 2021, I was intubated. Being in a coma, for me, felt like how some people have described feeling drugged. I could hear things going on, but I couldn't really see them. It was confusing. It's almost like you're in a different place. I remember hearing ladies saying, "I feel so bad for her because she has three kids at home, and she's really pretty."

At some point while I was in my coma, I thought I was on the back of an 18-wheeler and the driver was contemplating dropping me off after he killed me. Because of that, I kept trying to tell him that I had three kids and to not kill me. I'm a big fan of *Grey's Anatomy*, and in one scene, I remember one of the doctors telling the gunmen her life story in hopes he would feel bad and let her live. So, I decided to do that, too. I would always try to hold up the number three so they would correlate that with the number of kids I had.

Over the next few days, I bounced around from city to city (all in my head) and somehow now, I'm in New York. I can finally open my eyes and I'm not in the same hospital I was taken to. I wake up to see a nurse going through my plastic personal bag, admiring my shoes and saying, "Well we're just going to throw them in the trash." I have a big window and there is nothing but tall buildings. Another nurse comes in asking me questions, and the first thing I say or try to say is, "Where are my kids?"

My throat is very dry, and nothing is coming out. So she gives me a pen and paper. For some reason, my hands aren't working. It's hard to communicate because the staff members are walking around in what look to be spacesuits, and I can't get words out. They let my daughter call, but it's on speaker phone. So I can't tell her that they are lying to her. I'm not in the same hospital as they are telling her. I'm in New York and they are experimenting on me, just like they did in Tuskegee. I don't want to tell her because they have all of my information and can easily kill her and her brothers. This makes me depressed and withdrawn, and on top of all that, I'm seeing and hearing things!! In one of my hallucinations, the doctor is the president, so I'm screaming, "I voted for you, why would you do this to me? Why would you take me from my kids?" The nurses give me something, and then I start seeing chickens dance in my room.

All of these things convince me that they are just going to kill me since I won't concede and let them do their experiment. I feel I will never see my kids again and that pain was too much to bear. I would plead and beg the nurses to just kill me. I would ask them to give me some type of medicine that would allow me to just die. I did not want to chance them killing my kids too, so I figured I would just end it right then and save my kids.

I could feel my kids' energy, too, so I spoke on that to each of them as I said my goodbyes to them individually. For my oldest, I felt him being tired, so my goodbye to him was, "Stay strong a little while longer son. I know it'll be hard at first, but eventually you will find peace. You are the oldest, and I need you to take care of your brother and sister. I love you so much."

For my daughter, I felt the spirit of her giving up, so my goodbye to her was "Keep fighting Toot. You have always been stronger than you realize, and Mommy needs you to stay with your brothers because they won't listen to no one else. I love you so much."

For my baby, I felt a lot of sadness. His goodbye was, "It's okay, Stank. Don't be sad because I will always be in your heart. I will go wherever you go, like your personal angel. Listen to your brother and sister. I love you."

My mind was made up. If the nurses wouldn't do it, I was going to do it myself. I tried to kill myself three times by taking my oxygen mask off. I was extubated, but I still required a large amount of oxygen. In movies when people die, I've always seen their spirits go up, but I would always go backwards, like through a tunnel. I would go through forests and cities and end up in front of this big, black mass. The black mass reminded me of the movie *Hellraiser*. It was a big mass with bloodshot red eyes and pins sticking out of it. It never moved or made a sound, but I could feel it being happy to see me, except the last time.

The third time was different. My body felt like it was releasing. I remember thinking "dying isn't that bad." I was ready to go so that I could give my kids some peace and begin the healing process. As I made my way through the path heading towards "Pinhead," I heard my name being called. To this day, I still don't know who it was, but it was in the distance that someone was calling my name. I felt a spirit of peace and lightness. I then changed my mind about going to see "Pinhead." It still never said a word or moved, but the energy coming from it felt angry. I didn't care. I wanted to see who was calling me.

I woke up in my hospital room coughing, and the nurses coming in telling me to keep my oxygen on. They ended up taping the tube in place so that it couldn't be removed. After that, the story of Job came to me. I then knew that God wasn't going to allow me to die and that the devil was trying me in the form of COVID. COVID presented itself to me in different forms, and I cursed them and fought them in my dreams and in reality. Because of my combativeness, the nursing staff was not as friendly and helpful and began to mistreat me.

One night, I stayed on the bedpan for four hours because they no longer answered my calls. I pressed on and dealt with the mistreatment because I had faith that I was going to get out of that place soon. The dreams were different then. When I dreamed about my kids, I saw pink and blue surrounding them like they were happy and having a party. Days later I was transferred to the step-down unit where the hallucinations stopped, and my care was better. I then found out that I had been intubated for eight days, and the doctors were questioning if I would ever come off the ventilator. My phone had numerous messages and texts praying for me and encouraging me not to give up. My friends and family must have known that I needed all of that energy because it was their love and hope, along with God, that helped me survive. I spent a total of three and a half weeks hospitalized and came home with oxygen and the need for physical therapy due to being on bedrest the entire time.

Before I got sick, I needed four classes to complete my bachelor's degree. This was the time to do it since I was out of work on disability for rehabilitation. Things weren't easy. I still couldn't walk to the mailbox without getting tired, and I always had chest pains. COVID left me with a high heart rate, depression, anxiety, and PTSD. I can recall falling asleep with the television on and waking up halfway outside because I heard voices and thought that I was back being held hostage. PTSD is why I can tell my story as if it happened yesterday because there hasn't been a day since I was discharged that something hasn't reminded me of my ordeal. There was a time when I was going through a situation with my son who suffers from a chronic illness. I questioned God and asked him, "Why me?"

As sure as I am sitting here typing this, God answered me and said, "Why not you? Why not go through a trial and get through it so that you can tell the world about what I can do?" My experience with COVID is not just a story about the pandemic, but a story of faith, strength, and a will to live. I'm not a saint, a regular church goer, or someone who can quote scriptures on demand. But I am a woman who knows and loves God, and He knows and loves me back.

After being discharged and having my family fill in the blanks of my illness with the knowledge I have on my own, I know that I have a specific purpose that I have yet to reach. Maybe it's being a part of this book and telling my story so that another small-town girl who sometimes feels inadequate can know. It doesn't matter who writes you off when God is the author of your story. I say to you, whenever your world seems to fall apart, remember to give God the praise, close your eyes and just breathe.

Mothers & Daughters Anthology II

About the Author

Shandrika Milligan

Shandrika Milligan, a mother of three, was born in a small town outside of Columbia, SC. She holds an associate degree in applied science from Midlands Technical College as well as a Bachelor of Science Degree from Columbia International University. In her free time, Shandrika enjoys traveling and being an amateur food critic.

Dedication

I dedicate this chapter to my husband, Dru. He has cheered me on since day one and has always challenged me to be me, without reservations, as the person God created me to be. He sees me and has often said that I have so much to offer girls and women of all ages. For years, I didn't believe that, but he has. Now that I'm showing up as myself, I can see a bit more clearly.

Longing to Belong

By Sabrina R. Owens

"For everything there is a season, a time for every activity under heaven. A time to be born and a time to die. A time to plant and a time to harvest. A time to kill and a time to heal. A time to tear down and a time to build up. A time to cry and a time to laugh. A time to grieve and a time to dance. A time to scatter stones and a time to gather stones. A time to embrace and a time to turn away. A time to search and a time to quit searching. A time to keep and a time to throw away. A time to tear and a time to mend. A time to be quiet and a

time to speak. A time to love and a time to hate. A time for war and a time for peace. What do people really get for all their hard work? I have seen the burden God has placed on us all. Yet God has made everything beautiful for its own time. He has planted eternity in the human heart, but even so, people cannot see the whole scope of God's work from beginning to end. So, I concluded there is nothing better than to be happy and enjoy ourselves as long as we can. And people should eat and drink and enjoy the fruits of their labor, for these are gifts from God."
Ecclesiastes 3:1-13 NLT

Where do I start?

For as long as I can remember, I've always wanted to fit in and be accepted. I've always wanted to be noticed and applauded. Maybe it's an innate human desire. Maybe it's an unhealthy cry for attention. Or maybe both.

I grew up in the Lowcountry of South Carolina, in a small town called Saint Stephen. It's about 50 miles north of Charleston. I lived there with my parents in a single-wide trailer off a very long dirt road, near a golf course. The most distinct thing I remember about that house is the bright red carpet. My dad was a local mechanic, and my mom worked at an industrial plant in town. We had a pretty decent life…I think.

I remember as far back when there were three of us: my two brothers and me. My dad was incarcerated. When I was four years old, my mom, brothers, and I were in my grandfather's old wood-paneled station wagon on our way to visit with my dad. Upon backing out of the driveway, my one-year-old brother fell out of the car; I'm not sure if he was in a car seat. I remember my mom screaming and running to get help, but it was too late. He was not breathing.

The days ahead were so grim. I don't recall crying, but the sadness that filled the air was like a choking smoke, especially for my mom. I'm not sure if she ever recovered, because looking back, she always seemed sad. My dad was allowed to attend the funeral. I remember looking up and seeing him at the gravesite with a shovel in his hands, and his face was covered in tears.

Now there were only two of us, and we spent many summers with our great aunt in McClellanville, South Carolina. She was everything! Over time, our trips there became more frequent. The overnight stays got longer, but I didn't mind…I loved being there. I preferred it.

Chaos...or normal?

My parents' marriage was pretty turbulent, back and forth with one another for the next few years, even up until I was in second grade. One Saturday morning, through a mob of tears, my very pregnant mom began packing clothes, dishes, books, and anything else she could. My parents had separated, and we went to stay with my great aunt, until well after my mom had my younger sister...just one month after Hurricane Hugo.

Sometime later, my mom went back to work, yet we were a bit everywhere. Sometimes we stayed in McClellanville. Sometimes we stayed with friends in Shulerville. Sometimes we stayed with other friends in Pineville. Over the years, I'd hear whispers from my family members, speaking so ill about my mother, even calling her stupid. I'd break inside every time, wishing I were "bigger" so that I could speak up for her. I always wanted to defend her honor but thought I'd get in trouble because of it. They could be so mean and didn't care about the fact that I was in their presence, taking it all in. It was crushing!

Eventually, my brother and I lived primarily with our dad, but I longed to be with our mother. It was a challenge because she wasn't as financially stable as my dad was. As a teenager, I became so defiant and even thought I had the right to be…all because I didn't want to be with my dad. Surely, he provided, so we didn't want for anything. But I often had a silent distaste towards him, and I *internally* blamed him for my mom's sadness and instability. I would call her whenever my dad would not let me "have my way." I even asked her, "Can I just run away?" I just missed her so much.

Heartbreak...

Finally, my mom had a place of her own! When I was in tenth grade, my dad took a contract job out of town. That year, I lived with my mom and sister. It was glorious!!! My brother stayed with our aunt and uncle nearby. I savored that time with her. Our simple lives together were magic! Every evening, we'd walk out to see if her pink four o'clock flowers had bloomed. She seemed most content in the mundane, such as tilling the soil in her flower bed each Saturday morning. Dinner was always something simple and savory. I had longed for this consistency with her, so much so that I felt the need to add "ma'am" when addressing her. I needed her to know that I missed her deeply.

One night, my mom said that she wasn't going to work the next day and wrote down instructions for my sister and me. I was told to ride the bus home to my dad's, and he would bring me back to her house later that evening. As the time ticked, my mother didn't come home by the time that she said she would. I anxiously began watching the news, just to see if there was a report of something happening to her. My sister cried all night until she fell asleep; I was not sure why.

After midnight, there was a knock at the door. It was the most bizarre picture…my dad on the porch, my uncle standing nearby, and the couple who owned the convenience store in front of the house. My dad told me to pack our clothes and come on with him. It was so strange. I told him that I wanted to stay and wait for mom. I insisted. He looked so defeated, and calmly said it again. I firmly told him no. Through very sad eyes, he told me that our mother was dead. I dropped to the floor. I had never experienced such a wound. My heart was literally pounding. My ears were throbbing. My entire body felt warm. I sobbed myself into utter exhaustion. A car accident.

I'm the oldest of my siblings. At fifteen, I automatically assumed the role of mom and big sister. I "had" to grow up pretty fast. I learned how to cook, buy groceries, pay bills, drive, work, etc. I tried incredibly hard and thought I was doing a decent job. I remember a high school friend asked me "How do you do it?" Anytime I'd get that question, my response was always, "I got to be strong for my brother and sister." It wasn't until about twelve years later where I learned that none of that was my responsibility. I wasn't supposed to assume a role of such great magnitude…a parent; I was just a kid myself. But I thought it was normal.

Away from home...

I didn't start thinking about college until my senior year of high school. A friend told me to apply, so I did, and got accepted to USC Upstate. Honestly, it was lonely and my first time away from home. I started a job at the local mall. While working there, I met a young lady who was *just different*: jovial, super nice, and very stylish! She invited me to church with her, and it was the first time I tuned into the fact that Jesus is coming back. Say what? Talk about mind blown! I always considered myself a nice person, popular, and friendly. However, the fact that I was fornicating with my boyfriend made me think otherwise. I tried hard to rationalize it with the fact that we loved each other and planned to get married. But the Lord pricked my heart over and over again.

Around age 19, I began walking with Jesus, and life has been challenging since then. My greatest struggles were sex, partying, and friends. To me, being a Christian meant "playing" the part. I had to look a certain way, speak a certain way, and act a certain way…like overnight! I was super hard on myself because I was not like the women I went to church with. They seemed to have it all together. If asked, "How are you doing?" their response was always, "I'm blessed and highly favored!" I didn't "feel" blessed and highly favored. I struggled inwardly with guys, loneliness, finances, roommates, and grades. I was being taught that Christianity is evident when you're flourishing, and when you have no sin in your life. It seemed like I needed more faith, so I began studying and listening to songs about faith. If I believed hard enough, then all my troubles would be over…right? Needless to say, my beginnings were rooted in a prosperity gospel, where my works would get me into heaven. I began associating with other believers who tooted their own horns and looked down on others who weren't as fine-tuned in their appearance or their walk with God. Birds of a feather…! At least I looked well-polished on the outside. However, I craved more on the inside. I needed the truth.

Darkest hour…

In my third year of college, I moved into an apartment with two young ladies. It seemed great at first, but I bit off much more than I could chew. It wasn't a good choice financially and things got very tense. I didn't have my rent on time, more than once, and my roommates did not relent. It was so bad to where I hated being home. And when I was, I stayed locked in my room.

I remember coming from church one night, and I sat in my car before heading up the stairs of my apartment building. I was listening to songs of praise, but crumbling within, desperately crying out to God for financial help. It was agonizing. Was God there? Did I have "enough" faith? I just needed relief.

A group of teenagers from church began to flock towards me. It was nice to have them look up to me; I hoped for the right reasons. I had them over for a weekend, and we had a blast! I would often braid my own hair, and one of the girls, Shundra, saw it. She begged her mom, Ms. Vanessa, for the same style and asked me to do it. The technique is a long process, so they invited me over after church. I was happy to oblige, because that meant I didn't have to go home, at least not right away. I avoided that apartment at all costs. I braided Shundra's hair into the evening and ended up staying overnight. It was a relief!

The next morning, Ms. Vanessa had left early for work. I was preparing to go back home to get ready for class, and Shundra asked me to take her to school. On the way there, she said, "Ma said to call her." Perplexed, I said "Okay." After dropping Shundra off, I had a fleeting thought of "What if she asks me to stay with her?" So, I called Ms. Vanessa on the way home and she said, "I don't like the situation you're in with your roommates… I've prayed about it, and I've talked to the girls about it, and we want to know if you want to come live with us. I don't want anything from you. I just want you to finish school." Jesus!!! Seriously???

Upon moving in, I asked Ms. Vanessa what I should call her? What's crazy is I knew the answer before she responded, and I was already content with it. With a huge smile, she said "Ma." So, for the last 20 years, she's been affectionately known as my godmother and Whitney and Shundra are my god sisters! I literally gained an entire family! To me, I was five years in limbo, and Vanessa picked up where Delores, my mom, left off. She taught me money management, work ethic, and, by example, being a God-fearing woman. It was the first time in my adult life where I had community and began to learn to just be myself. I was seen and I was loved. Sweet relief!!!

"Get all the advice and instruction you can, so you will be wise the rest of your life."

Proverbs 19:20 NLT

GREATEST struggle...

Men!!! They were my greatest struggle...before Jesus, and certainly after!

Surely, I've always wanted someone to like me for me, and who only wanted me. But there were also times that I lived pretty frivolously. Before salvation, I didn't think anything was wrong with it, because I was getting the attention that I wanted. I never thought of it as promiscuity, or that it was unbecoming. However, after salvation, I got a glimpse of how much God loved me, and I felt conviction with every encounter of every man afterwards. Romantic relationships became such a challenge now that I had a conscious, a filter, awareness, The Holy Spirit! Yes, I ignored most of those red flags because I was still trying to live life as I once did. Only now, I thought that if they hung around me long enough, I'd be a godly influence on them.

Obviously, I was far in over my head and succumbed to every temptation. I thought that I was "strong enough" to pull them up, yet I was always sinking. I compromised, rationalized, and even gave myself over into clear foolishness, all because I thought it was the best that I could get…thinking that it would not affect me spiritually. Was being unequally yoked really a thing? There was a time where I even feared for my life! Although I was never physically hit, I saw signs where it could have gone that route, and I ignored them all because I was getting the attention that I wanted…at least I thought I wanted. This guy was erratic, territorial, and calloused. He looked at me as if I were property, instead of a person, always questioning where I was and who I was with. Once, his pregnant ex-girlfriend came over, beating and banging on the outside of his home, screaming for him to come outside. It went on for over an hour, and I laid there scared, sad for her and for myself. Why am I here? Why am I doing this to myself? My car was trashed in the process, and he laughed it off. I was done.

There were a few more relationships after that whirlwind. After so many heart, mind, and body compromises, I gave up. Surely, life had to be better than this! While finishing school at Charleston Southern University, I remember walking on campus in the middle of the day saying, "Lord, I'm sorry. I really want to be in a godly relationship with someone who wholeheartedly loves You. I'm tired of putting myself through unnecessary chaos. I always get too far ahead of myself. I want to wait on You. Help me to focus on what's in front of me, which is finishing school. This is hard to say, but I am going to wait on You. Amen." Being that honest with God was excruciating, but His peace flooded me immediately. And so, I minded my business and focused on school.

The CHAMP is here!

School was going very well! I had a work-study job at the campus post office and was working full-time at a hotel. Looking back, I don't know how I managed to do all three gracefully! But I did. I had a coworker from India who was headed home to visit his family for a few weeks. He needed someone to take over for his overnight shift while he was gone. So, I did. Working third shift at a hotel, you'll witness some of the craziest things! However, I had a lot of downtime to read and study.

In January of 2009, while minding my business (on Facebook), I saw that I had a friend request...from some guy. Oh God...who the heck was this? So, I accepted...to be nosey. I opened up the chat box saying:

"Hey!" I don't know who you are, but "Hey!" He responded, and we've been talking ever since then. It was nice to finally just talk to someone about life, interests, school, family, etc. For weeks, we chatted on Facebook. Then, he shared his phone number. I wanted to call, but it took me a while because I liked him a lot and didn't want to get too far ahead of myself. What if he just wants to be friends? God, help me! I remember telling my BFF about him, that I liked him. She looked at me and said, "Just tell him!" As simple as that was; it was colossal. I had NEVER told someone that I liked them! But I took the plunge.

"Hey! I know you gave me your number to call you, and I want to. It's just that I have often gotten way ahead of myself with guys. The problem is that I REALLY like you…as more than a friend.

He responded, "Good, because I like you too!"

I finally called him. It was so weird because I felt like a giddy schoolgirl...a 27-year-old schoolgirl. But I relaxed when he laughed at my joke. It was so freeing to just be myself! I didn't have to walk on eggshells or play a part to impress; he just liked me for me! So, we officially began courting in March 2009 and met in person two months later. Our relationship spanned one and a half years. He was finishing school in Pennsylvania, and I was finishing in South Carolina. One month after he graduated, we got married. Certainly, not normal, but definitely lovely. Yes, he's my champion!

Life is not linear...

Life is not what I expected it to be. None of this was planned...by me, at least. It has been a hard, yet very good work. Marriage and family are not what we read in books or see in movies. It is definitely not a fairytale. It requires constant effort, dying to myself daily, praying earnestly for my husband and children, and for myself to keep choosing Christ. I must say that in this daily grind, God has blessed us with community, to spur us on in Him.

As much as I'm learning, it is certainly stretching me in ways I never knew I needed, even requiring me to make the hard, not-so-ordinary decisions, especially when it comes to raising our children. This world can be distracting, even with the things that seem necessary and good. I attempt to be in constant communion with God, so that what's loud around me doesn't deter me. Nor does it define me. *"And so, dear brothers and sisters, I plead with you to give your bodies to God because of all he has done for you. Let them be a living and holy sacrifice—the kind he will find acceptable. This is truly the way to worship him. Don't copy the behavior and customs of this world, but let God transform you into a new person by changing the way you think. Then you will learn to know God's will for you, which is good and pleasing and perfect." Romans 12:1-2 NLT*

    Our upbringing massively shapes who we are, to the point where we sometimes think that our way is the right and only way. We make plans of what our lives will become, and maybe it comes to fruition just as expected. However, that's very rare. We get so caught up in the glory, but don't realize the weighty responsibilities of such high regard. We want the badge of honor but don't want to do the required work. We think we want such stature, but do we really know what we're asking for?

Do we count the cost? Again, nothing in my life has gone the way I expected it to. "Straight and narrow" seems easy. Set the goals and execute them, right? Straight seems obtainable, but I forgot about the narrow, which introduced me to all the twists and turns that come along with it. There are a multitude of off roads and beaten paths! *"You can make many plans, but the Lord's purpose will prevail." Proverbs 19:21 NLT*

Still Loading...

"What do you want to be when you grow up?" It's a loaded question that every child is asked by an adult. And from there, our brains begin to form the life of the ideal "American dream." It's where I remember dreaming about my "perfect," easy, care-free life…filled with ALL the things and people that I love. Sometimes, I wish I knew me before those ideas began to form in my brain. Who was I before that? It's funny how life and people can easily, and very early, cause us to think that we are not good enough and we should want to be better. What's sad is that the "better" is always superficial, of no substance, and not authentic. Oh, how beautiful it would be, if we knew early on and grasped how much The Savior loves us AS WE ARE!

My life is not measured by the hats I've worn, my accomplishments, my skills, or my successes. Neither is my life measured by my many failures. Regardless of it all, The Lord knew me and loved me before the foundations of the world. I really wish I knew of His love towards me then. Maybe I would have taken a different route? It's possible. Regardless of the direction, our Father's love extends farther and wider than our finite minds can fathom. There is no place we can run that He can't reach. There is no tragedy too monumental that He cannot expunge. Even when we make the unfavorable choice, He is able to work it together for His glory.

Every day, I wrestle with something. Such is life! However, knowing that I'm fiercely loved as I am gives me courage to journey on. When I "grow up," I'm content with just being me. No bells and whistles, platforms, hats, or badges of honor…just me. And that is enough!

"The faithful love of the Lord never ends! His mercies never cease. Great is his faithfulness; his mercies begin afresh each morning. I say to myself, 'The Lord is my inheritance; therefore, I will hope in him!'"
Lamentations 3:22-24 NLT

Mothers & Daughters Anthology II

About the Author

Sabrina R. Owens

Sabrina R. Owens grew up in a very small town near Charleston, SC. After high school, she began college at USC Upstate in Spartanburg, SC and majored in education. While there, a coworker invited her to church, and this is where her life and love for Christ began. Through that church, she met a family that wanted to "adopt" her as their own. For over 20 years, they're still affectionately known as her family.

In 2009, Sabrina finished her undergrad degree at Charleston Southern University, with a major in religion, and minors in psychology and education. Soon after, she met (on Facebook!) and married her champion, Andrew/Dru. They have three littles...Mathias, Blythe, and Ziva. Some of their favorite times include movie nights, a competitive game of UNO, random drives around the city (or beyond), gathering with friends, and telling corny jokes!

Her daily reminder:

"Don't copy the behavior and customs of this world, but let God transform you into a new person by changing the way you think. Then you will learn to know God's will for you, which is good and pleasing and perfect."
Romans 12:2

Mothers & Daughters Anthology II

Dedication

This chapter is dedicated to the One Whom is the basis and reason for all I do—Jesus Christ. In Him I live and move and have my being.

Rusty's Restoration

By Annette Beggarly

My husband stood at death's door repeatedly. Jesus wouldn't let the enemy take him. COVID was relentless when it first reared its ugly head in 2020 and 2021. During the last week of July and into the first week of August of the latter year, COVID became a beast that moved into our lives with all the fury hell could muster.

First, our granddaughter, Ariel, (who lives with us) came down with it. Three days after she got sick, I contracted the virus; and three days after that, my husband, Rusty, followed suit. I had pneumonia, but Ariel and I recovered. Rusty was not as fortunate. He got worse and worse until his pulse oximetry revealed that his oxygen level was down to sixty-eight percent. Our son, who is director of nursing at a large hospital, told me that we needed to get his dad to an emergency room ASAP. (He told me later that if we had not rushed him to the hospital, in all probability, he would have died at home that night.)

I took Rusty to a nearby hospital, walked into the emergency room, and told the lady at the desk that my husband had COVID and was very sick. I told her that he was unable to walk from the car to the door. A couple medical personnel came out to our car with a wheelchair and helped him into the hospital. I was told that due to COVID protocol, I would not be able to go back with him. We lived eighteen minutes from the hospital. I told the staff I would go home and wait for them to call me. I left. Little did I know what the future held... Rusty was able to call me himself after several hours. He told me they were not able to treat COVID patients at this hospital, and they were transferring him to a bigger hospital that was an hour away.

Later that night, Rusty was transported to Virginia's Lynchburg General Hospital and admitted. Thus began an emotional rollercoaster of highs and lows that were one minute exhilarating and the next, excruciating. Throughout the whole ordeal, I had no clue what would come next. Rusty was in the regular part of the hospital for a couple days, but things got progressively worse. So he had to be moved into ICU and put on a ventilator.

I am employed at New Life Community Church in Danville, Virginia. The phone call telling me that Rusty was going to be put on a ventilator came just as we were beginning our staff meeting that day. The doctor told me that, unfortunately, this would be the beginning of a long, hard road for him. We had no idea at that time just how hard it would be. I had the doctor on speaker. My pastor's wife, Steph, told me to ask to speak to Rusty. Looking back, I am so very grateful she suggested that. They put Rusty on the phone. He was very weak and barely able to talk. I did not know at that moment if it would be the last time I would ever hear his voice. Jesus knew I would need my coworkers at that time. We spent two and a half hours praying for Rusty that day after the ominous phone call. The staff at New Life are incredible people who are beautifully dedicated to God and to their parishioners. They are entirely sincere and would walk through fire for the dear souls who are a part of our church and entrusted to their care.

I wasn't allowed to see Rusty when he was on the COVID floor at Lynchburg General, so Pastor Steph went with my family and me to stand on the sidewalk outside the hospital and pray for Rusty.

Our son, Russell; our grandson, Atticus: our granddaughter, Ariel; our son, Jonathan; me; our daughter, Leslie; our daughter-in-law, Kayla; and our grandson, Gideon

Mothers & Daughters Anthology II

My pastor's wife, Steph, and me

When all this began, I was still administrator for New Life. I had been offered the position of children's pastor, and I was beginning to move into that role. I was researching curricula for the coming year. I had decided on one, but the enemy of our souls told me he fully intended on stopping me from leading our children to Jesus. He vehemently did not want me to be used for the Kingdom of God in that manner. He told me matter-of-factly, "If you order that curriculum, I WILL KILL your husband."

I talked to our lead pastor, Jim Reed, about this. He told me, "Annette, you cannot negotiate with a terrorist. The devil is a terrorist. If you do what he says, he will kill you anyway." Fast–forward a couple days, and Jesus set it up so that Pastor Steph and I were in the office together at the same time when I was ready to order the curriculum. I had filled out the form online and put in the credit card information. I was getting ready to hit the submit button. I told Steph that this is where I was in the order process and asked her if we could pray before I hit that button. We prayed together, sang to Jesus and praised Him. We spent some time doing that, and, BOOM, I hit the button.

It was, literally, about two minutes later when the doctor called me from the hospital and gave me one of the worst reports we had gotten. We just kind of looked at each other in silence for a bit, and Steph said, "Annette, I thought we would get a worse report before we got a better one."

Pastor Jim held a night of worship after this for all of us to praise God in the face of the enemy on behalf of Rusty and a man named Roddey (who also had COVID and was going through many of the same things Rusty was). We were warring on behalf of some others we knew who needed healing, as well. We did this declaring the might and power of our Almighty God—believing for healing for those who needed it.

So, just like God told Joshua to march around the city seven times and He would give him victory over Jericho, Pastor Steph and I marched around the tech booth (located toward the back of our sanctuary) seven times during this service believing for victory in the lives of those who needed healing. 1 Corinthians 1:25 says, "For the foolishness of God is wiser than human wisdom, and the weakness of God is stronger than human strength." You know, what looks like foolishness to some people is actually obedience to God. Steph and I were willing to do whatever God told us to in order to lay claim to the promised healings we knew God had given us. It was that night when a dear older man who is on our council at New Life

(Frank McDaniel) prophesied that Rusty was going to not only pull through, but that he was going to fully recover and go back to work.

The next Sunday, Pastor Steph told me that she had a vision of Rusty walking into our church. Several people told me that they had visions of Rusty and me walking on the beach together. I held on to Frank's and Steph's words and the other prophecies with every grain of hope I could muster. I wanted Rusty to live more than I wanted to live myself.

Rusty was in COVID ICU for two weeks. As I said, I wasn't allowed to see him while he was there. A lady in our church, Cassandra Crump, contacted me and said that she had heard at the beginning of COVID that a doctor said his patients did better when they could hear their loved ones' voices. She told me she had a mini-recorder and asked if I would like to use it. I recorded my voice declaring healing scriptures over Rusty, praying over him, and just talking to him. The nurses would lay the recorder on his chest and play it for him. He was hearing my voice in spite of the fact that I couldn't be there, physically. I am convinced that God used this as part of his healing.

During a Wednesday afternoon prayer time at the church, Pastor Jim gave out sheets of paper that were full of healing scriptures. It was these scriptures that I read to Rusty on the recorder. These scriptures were my LIFE'S BLOOD throughout the whole ordeal. The papers ended up tattered and worn because I declared them over Rusty again and again. We got together as a family and declared them over him. Other members of our family declared them over Rusty repeatedly on their own.

These scriptures are available for you at the end of this chapter. I am telling you—they are priceless. Declare these scriptures over yourself and your family often. There is an amazing amount of power in these words, and they could mean the difference between life and death for you or someone you love.

At one point, I was in our bathroom at home. A pair of Rusty's shoes were on the floor near the sink. I accidentally dropped something, and it landed in one of his shoes. I wept and said out loud, "By God's grace, he WILL walk in these shoes again." I had made some extra copies of the healing scriptures, and I laid them in different places in our house on things that were Rusty's. I laid one of these papers on his shoes.

I also took some of these papers to the hospital, an ICU nurse met me downstairs, took the scriptures up to his room and put them on the table. I just wanted the Word of God to be near him. Every day Jesus would give me promise after promise from His Word when I would have my quiet time. I anointed Rusty's wedding band with oil and put it in the case it came in. Every day when God gave me a promise, I would lay his wedding band on my Bible in that particular spot where the scripture was and leave it there until the next time I began reading again. They termed Rusty "COVID Clear," meaning he wasn't contagious anymore, on August 19th, which was our 35th wedding anniversary. I wasn't expecting to see him that day. I drove to Lynchburg with the intention of giving the staff of the ICU donuts because it was our anniversary. I wrote scriptures on the donut box from Psalm 91.

The scriptures on the box were verses three and four which say, "Surely, He will save you from the fowler's snare and from the deadly pestilence. He will cover you with His feathers, and under His wings you will find refuge; His faithfulness will be your shield and rampart."

I took the donuts up to the outside of the entrance to the floor where Rusty was. A nurse came out to get them and told me if I would wait a bit, she would come back to get me so I could go in to see him. It just so happened they had called a "code blue" on a person, and I couldn't go in at that exact moment. Jesus did not cause that person to have that emergency, but He did use it to help me have time to gather my thoughts before I was able to see Rusty for the first time. I didn't know what he would look like. Jesus allowed me time to pray, and He brought so many comforting scriptures to my mind as I sat there and waited. This was to be Rusty's last day in COVID ICU. Since he was declared "COVID Clear," they told me that they would make an exception and allow me to come on the

COVID floor to be with him on our 35th wedding anniversary. The nurse came back to get me, and when I went onto the floor, they met me with a bouquet of flowers, a balloon and a card they had all signed. One of the nurses had made a banner to put on Rusty's door, so this is what I saw when I first got to the outside of his room…

Rusty's feet and legs are seen in the background. They told me I could go into his room. This is what he looked like when I went in...

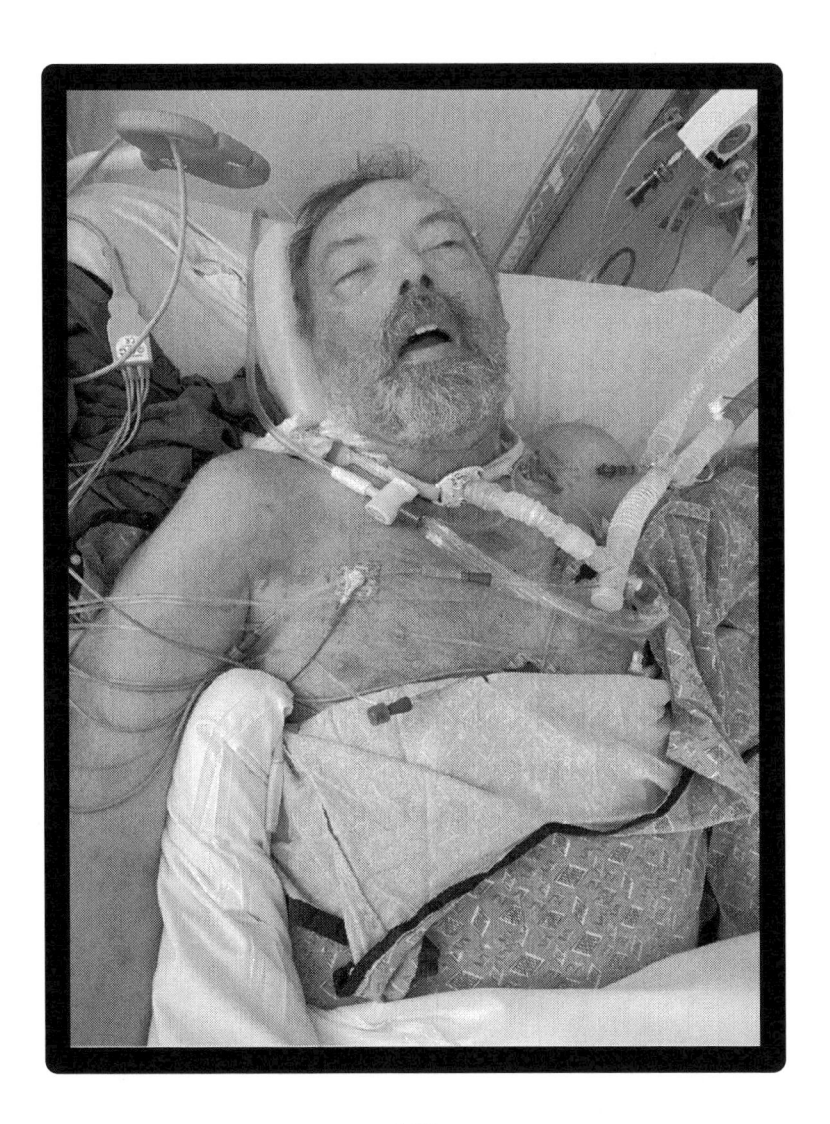

Rusty's arms were tied down in restraints. They kept him in restraints for weeks. I was able to spend some time with him, which was priceless to me. Rusty was unaware, physically or mentally, that I was there; but I have to believe that spiritually, we had a very intimate connection during that time. That night he was moved to a regular ICU. The maximum time for a person to be on a ventilator used to be two weeks, but since COVID happened, people were allowed three weeks before having to switch to something different.

Mothers & Daughters Anthology II

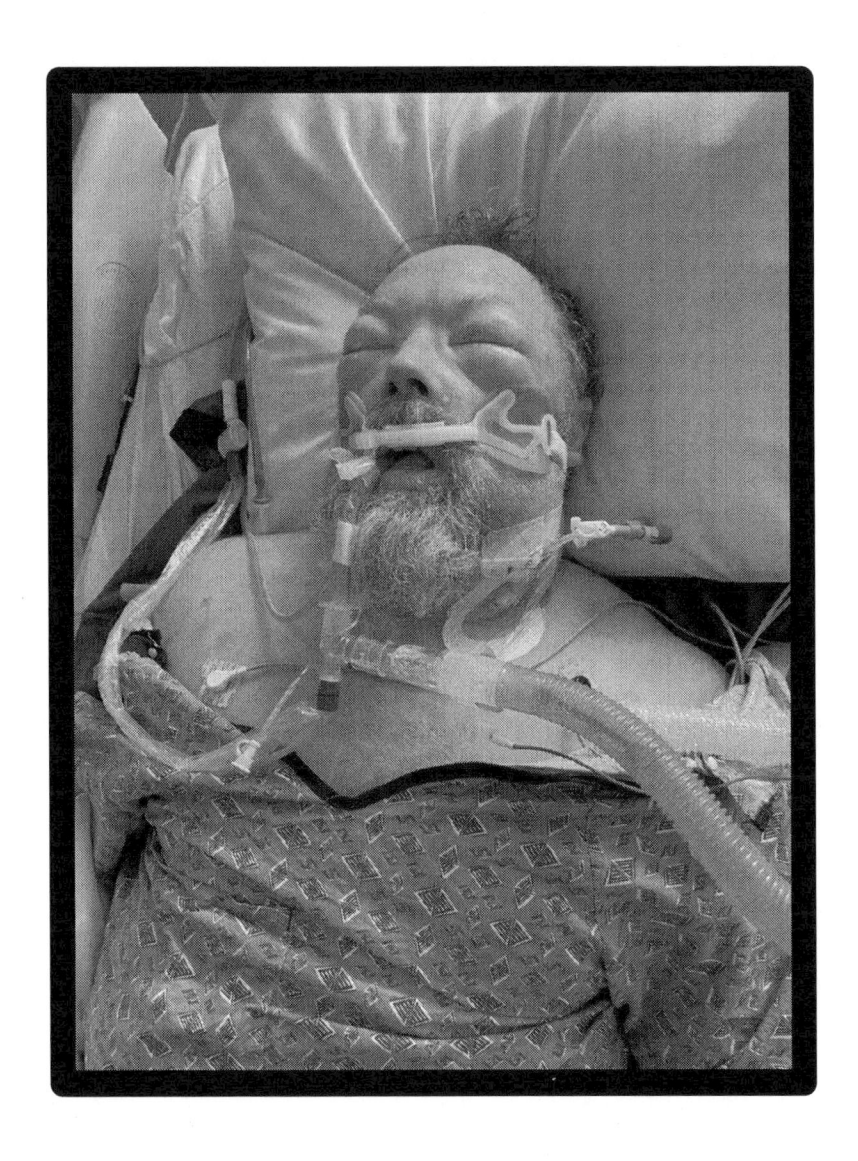

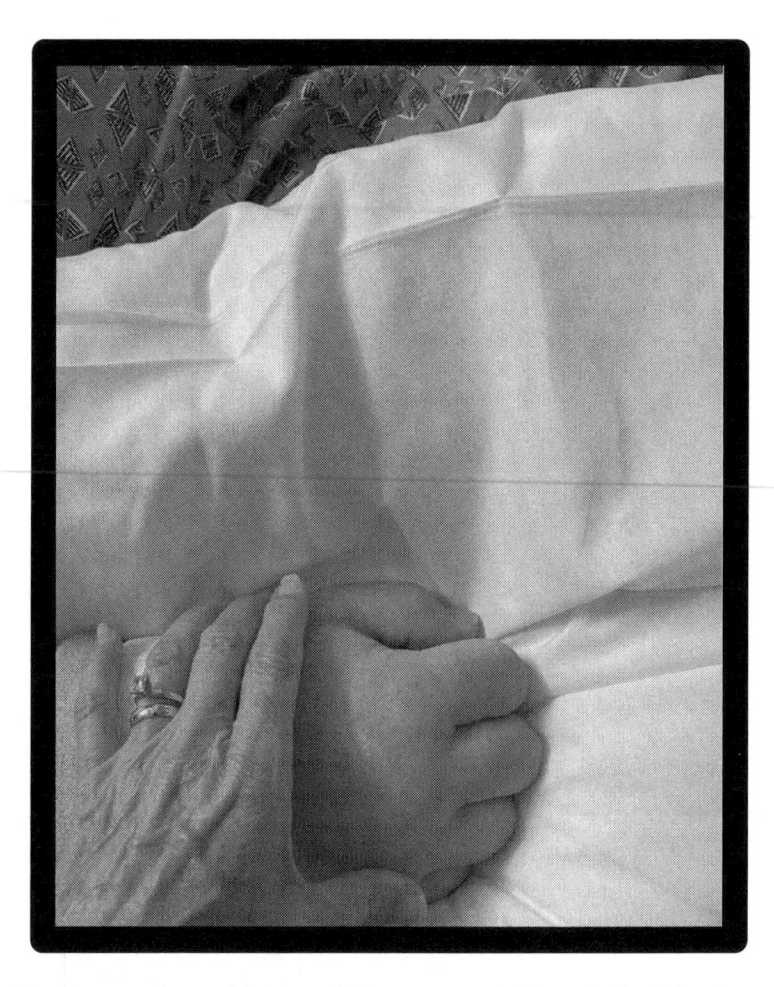

Rusty continued to swell because of the air that had to be pumped into his body.

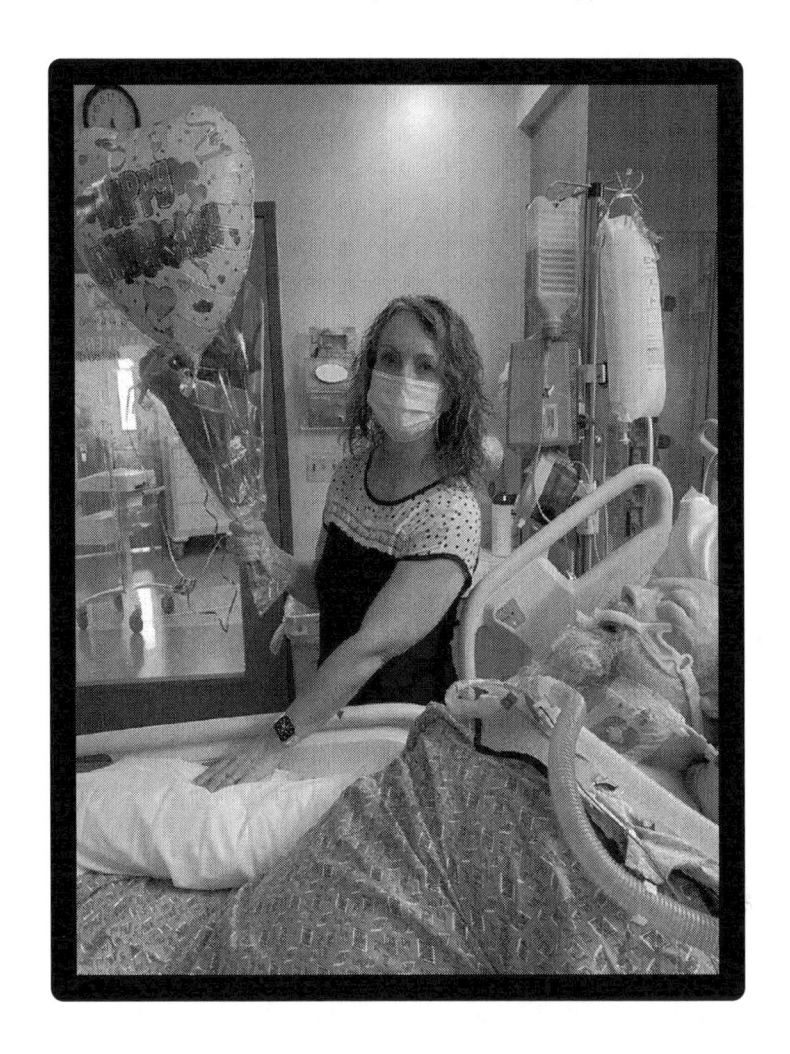

Rusty developed acute respiratory distress syndrome, which is very often deadly. This is how he looked then...

Still, after a few days, doctors said he had been on the vent too long, and they were willing to give him a trial run to see how he would do without it. They removed the vent on August 25th. It seemed like he was, indeed, getting better, and I was elated. After only two days, things nosedived again, his lung collapsed, and he had to be reintubated. The vent was down his throat and into his trachea, forcing air into his lungs yet again.

I sat by his bed with tears streaming down my face as I silently cried. After a few days, they put a monitor on his head to measure his brain activity. They also gave him an NG tube so he could be fed and receive medicine through his nose. His kidneys began to fail, so the medical personnel put a catheter in his neck so they could do dialysis on him. I had to sign a release form for that because there was no guarantee he would ever be able to live without dialysis.

Rusty was in the hospital for almost two and a half months, and he was in ICU for six weeks. His muscles began to waste away. My husband, who worked about sixty hours a week at a job that required physical strength and endurance before getting COVID, was wasting away to almost nothing.

On September 1st, the doctor began asking me about doing a trach and peg on him (a tracheotomy and a feeding tube that would be put through a hole in his stomach). The doctor said that this could prolong his life, but there was no guarantee of what quality of life he would have. He said Rusty may die, or he may make it through and be a vegetable for the rest of his life, unable to feed himself or ever get out of a bed. The doctor said there was a possibility he would recover, but nobody was giving me ANY guarantees. I was told that Rusty had a 50/50 chance either way.

It was at this point that I had to go to Rusty's place of employment and sign papers pertaining to my receiving his pension if he were to die. It all seemed so surreal.

Ultimately, I had to make the decision about the trach and peg. It was an EXCRUCIATING decision to make because I knew he would not want to live in a vegetative state—but—still—I had to give him the chance to live. They did the trach and peg on September 3rd. I had to go out of his room when they did it because it was a sterile procedure. This is what I saw when I came back in...

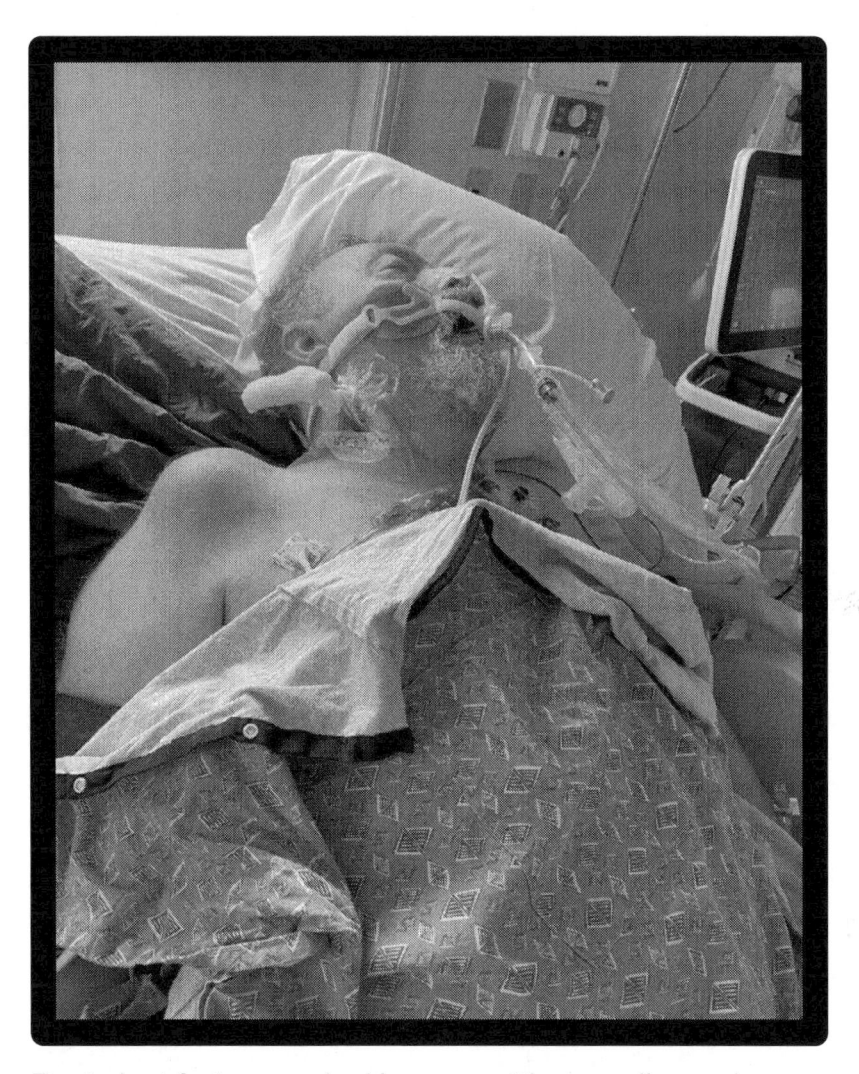

Rusty lost forty pounds. He was getting smaller and wrinkling.

I would sit in Rusty's room, watching his monitors as his blood pressure skyrocketed and then nosedived to nearly nothing—and I would grit my teeth and proclaim the power of our healing God over my husband's life. I would speak those healing scriptures out through clenched teeth in defiance against satan himself because I knew all of heaven had our backs. It was only the power of the blood of Jesus Christ that enabled me to do that. And I would pray and pray and pray some more. It was at this time when I talked to Pastor Jim and Steph on the phone. I had talked to them many times, but at this particular time Pastor Jim told me he was asking Jesus what He was speaking or praying over Rusty. He said Jesus gave him the word "Victory." He said that Jesus had told him we would be victorious in all this. I had no idea how it could happen, but here again, I held onto that word for dear life.

If you are a believer in Jesus Christ, you are needed to encourage and hold other believers up in their times of need. My pastor and his wife were there for us in so many ways during Rusty's battle against the enemy while he dealt with COVID and its aftereffects. Pastor Jim and Steph stood by our sides every minute. They spent an incredible amount of time praying. I am sure they lost sleep because of it. They pushed through against the enemy on our behalf and did so at personal expense. They encouraged me when everything seemed so dark and bleak. Rusty and I will be forever grateful to them for it all. You can be the hands and feet of Jesus, too. Never underestimate your ability to be there for your brothers and sisters in Christ.

Whenever my faith weakened, I proclaimed out loud over and over, "I TRUST YOU, GOD. I TRUST YOU WITH THIS. I TRUST YOU,

GOD." Shortly after Pastor Jim's giving me the word he got, I received the word, "WINNER." I believed He WOULD make it so we would win this war against the enemy of our souls. Yet, there were times when I felt so weary, and one of the precious attenders of our church encouraged me by sending scriptures or a song. I received encouraging words and prayers via texts, emails, or phone calls. Those scriptures, songs and prayers were my lifeline. Many of them brought meals or sent money for gas and food for the daily trips I made to Lynchburg. I cannot adequately express my gratitude to the wonderful people of New Life Community Church in Danville, Virginia. These precious souls showed me the love of God in tangible ways, and I needed it more than I could possibly say. So, thank you to them, and to you, dear reader, please pour out your love on the people God has placed in your life.

If you are reading this and do not have a community of fellow believers with whom to do life, I strongly encourage you to become part of a Bible-believing church. How priceless is it to have a church family to weep with you when you weep and rejoice with you when you are rejoicing? During Rusty's stay in the hospital, God spoke to us with signs and wonders.

One day I was driving down the road and the song "Rattle" by Elevation Worship was playing on the radio. A terrible storm was raging that day. All at once, a blinding streak of lightning went through the sky and a deafening clap of thunder sounded at the exact time the song screamed out "LIVE!" I was screaming "LIVE" with the song, too. It was like Jesus and I both were screaming out and commanding life for my husband. There was another time when my daughter, Leslie, and I were driving back from the hospital when all this began. It was one of the first trips of many I made to Lynchburg and back. It was nighttime, and we were talking about Rusty and how we were choosing to trust God in spite of all the unknowns. All of a sudden, a HUGE comet with a long tail flew across the night sky and went plummeting toward the earth.

Isaiah 40:26-28 says, "Lift up your eyes to the sky and see for yourself. Who do you think created the cosmos? He lit every shining star and formed every glowing galaxy and stationed them all where they belong. He has numbered, counted, and given everyone a name. They shine because of God's incredible power and awesome might; not one fails to appear! Why, then, O Jacob's tribes, would you ever complain? And my chosen Israel, why would you say, 'Yahweh isn't paying attention to my situation. He has lost all interest in what happens to me.' Don't you know? Haven't you been listening? Yahweh is the One and Only Everlasting God, the Creator of all you can see and imagine! He never gets weary or worn out. His intelligence is unlimited; he is never puzzled over what to do!"

These were only two of the many signs God gave us during our journey through hell. He reminded us repeatedly that He was still there, and He had a plan. So, Rusty began to improve somewhat, and it was decided by the hospital personnel to move him out of ICU and into a long-term acute care facility at Virginia Baptist Hospital. Rusty has no recollection of being in the hospital past the first couple of days before he was placed in ICU.

Have you guys ever heard the song "Then Came the Morning" by Bill Gaither? This song tells how Jesus went from Holy Saturday with no indication that there was any life in Him to Easter Sunday when He was resurrected from the dead. Some of the lyrics to the song are as follows:

"They all walked away, nothing to say, they'd just lost their dearest friend All that He said, now He was dead So this was the way it would end the dreams they had dreamed were not what they'd seemed Now that He was dead and gone The garden, the jail, the hammer, the nail How could a night be SO long?

THEN CAME THE MORNING

Night turned into day

The stone was rolled away Hope rose with the dawn THEN CAME THE MORNING

Shadows vanished before the sun Death had lost and life had won

For the morning had come

    WELL, on Saturday, September 18th, Rusty was still oblivious to the fact that he was even in the world. He was barely able to use his arms or legs or move in any significant way. The next day, Sunday, September 19th, was my first day to begin my role as children's pastor and be with the kids in that capacity. On that very day, Jesus rolled away the stone and resurrected my husband. When I went to the hospital after church, this is what I found...

    He was fully conscious and interacting with everyone. He required almost no supplemental oxygen. Soon after this, his trach was removed. Rusty got better and better each day. He was able to go outside for the first time on September 30th. He had not been outside since August 5th when he was admitted into the hospital.

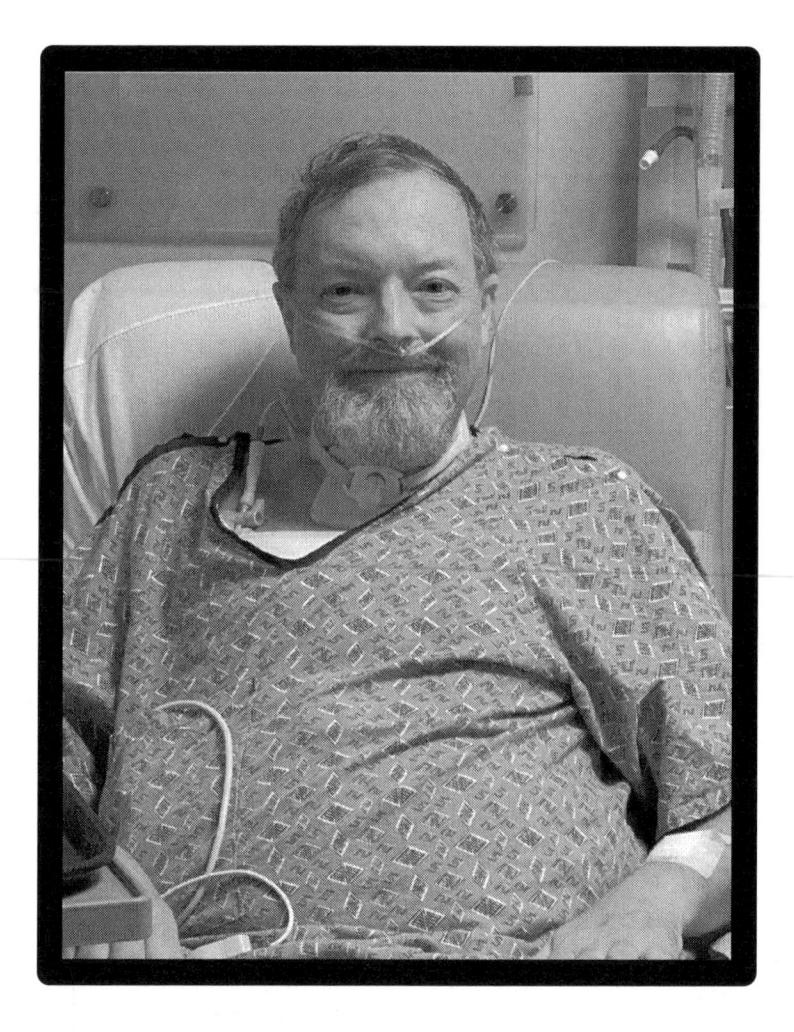

Rusty was sitting up and talking (with his trach still in—most people cannot talk with a trach).

Rusty outside for the first time, rocking that hospital gown!

Every time a doctor or nurse saw him (who had not seen him for a couple days prior to his resurrection day), he or she would say, "I cannot believe this is the same man." The hospital staff was totally amazed at his transformation.

Our son, Russell, who was the nursing director of a COVID Unit at Virginia's Roanoke Memorial Hospital at the time, said he had never seen anyone make that many strides and recover that quickly...and he has seen a lot of people suffer and die at the hands of COVID. Originally, staff had told me to expect Rusty to be in the hospital for seven months. They said he would have to go to a long-term acute care hospital, then to acute rehab, then home with Home Healthcare. Eventually he would go for physical therapy. Rusty was too advanced in his recovery to qualify for most of that.

Rusty and I left the hospital on October 13th, which was almost two and a half months from the first day he was admitted. He was able to begin right away with physical therapy.

We're leaving the hospital!

Goodbye hospital! Hello, world!

Mothers & Daughters Anthology II

About the Author

Annette Beggarly

Annette Beggarly lives in Danville, Virginia, with her husband, Rusty. She is Children's Pastor at New Life Community Church where she also leads Revelation Wellness Fitness classes. Annette enjoys spending time with her family and their Great Dane and German Shepherd. Her time in the quiet place with Jesus is the joy of her life. She will be eternally grateful to our Savior for giving her husband back to her. Every minute she spends with him is a priceless gift from God.

Epilogue

Rusty Beggarly has returned to work and is thriving. He has no complications from having been in the hospital for so long. He is in good health and is leading a wonderfully normal life again. To God be the glory forever and ever.

THIS WAS THE VICTORY OF GOD ALMIGHTY! Jesus won the victory over sin and death on that Sunday morning when He rose from the grave. He gave my husband back his life and defeated satan in the battle over our family and over children's ministry at New Life Community Church on that Sunday morning, September 19th. There was so much more that Jesus won with this battle! Yes, this was about my husband's life, but it was about so much more. It was about persevering in prayer until the answer came. Jesus taught us how to pray more fervently than we ever had. He taught us to give clock time to pressing in and praying through. It was about believing for healing and not letting go of that...NO MATTER WHAT. It was about our family's faith and the faith of generations to come. It was about our experiencing God's victory over satan in the most real and tangible way imaginable. It was about Jesus showing us that children's ministry is of the utmost importance. Matthew 8:14-17 says, "When Jesus came into Peter's house, he saw Peter's mother-in-law lying in bed with a fever. He touched her hand, and the fever left her; and she got up and began to wait on him. When evening came, many who were demon-possessed were brought to him, and he drove out the spirits with a word and healed all the sick. This was to fulfill what was spoken by the prophet Isaiah: 'He took up our infirmities and bore all our diseases.'"

JESUS CHRIST WANTS YOU TO KNOW THAT HE STILL HEALS TODAY! His power is unmatched! There is nothing in your life that is beyond His ability to heal! Do you have a problem? He has the answer! My husband was virtually given up for dead on several occasions, but God said, "NO!" God Almighty is available right now, right here to provide you with your healing. He has your miracle! The waters have been stirred, and He is inviting you in. There is nothing, absolutely nothing, He cannot do! If you have ANY request to lay before the Lord, whether it is physical, mental, emotional, spiritual, financial, or relational, please do not hold back. Pray bold prayers and expect the King of Kings to answer!

ALL PRAISE BE TO HIM WHO IS ABLE TO DO IMMEASURABLY MORE THAN WE COULD ASK OR IMAGINE. GLORY BE TO GOD!

Healing Declarations

1. By the stripes of Jesus, I am healed. He took my sickness; He carried my pain. I believe it is the will of God for me to be healed.

2. In the name of Jesus, I break every curse of infirmity, sickness and premature death off my body.

3. In the name of Jesus, I break every curse of witchcraft and destruction over my body from both sides of my family.

4. In the name of Jesus, I speak to every sickness in my body, and I command it to leave.

5. Every hidden sickness and every hidden disease, I command you to leave my body, in the name of Jesus.

6. I command all pain to leave my body, in the name of Jesus.

7. I speak to infections to come out of my body, in the name of Jesus.

8. I release miracles of healing in my body, in the name of Jesus.

9. I believe God for miracles of healing in my life and in my family wherever I go, in Jesus' name.

10. Thank you, Lord, for healing me and delivering me from all sickness and pain, in Jesus' name.

11. I speak to every condition. You must obey.

12. I speak to miracles, healings, signs and wonders. Be released into me, in Jesus' name.

13. I thank you, Lord, that health and healing are coming now.

14. Forgive me, Lord, for allowing any fear, guilt, self–rejection, self–hatred, sin, pride, unforgiveness, bitterness, and rebellion to open the door to any sickness or infirmity. I renounce these things, in the name of Jesus.

15. Jesus carried my sickness and infirmities.

16. I break all curses of sickness and disease, and I command all hereditary spirits of sickness to come out.

17. No sickness or disease shall come near my dwelling.

18. I command every germ or sickness that touches my body to die, in the name of Jesus.

19. I am redeemed from sickness and disease. I lose myself from every infirmity.

Healing Prayer

Scripture References

Psalm 107:20 (NLT)

He sent out his Word and healed them, snatching them from the door of death.

Isaiah 53:5 (NIV)

But he was pierced for our transgressions, he was crushed for our iniquities; the punishment that brought us peace was on him, and by his wounds we are healed.

1 Peter 2:24 (NIV)

"He, himself, bore our sins" in his body on the cross, so that we might die to sins and live for

righteousness; "by his wounds you have been healed."

Mark 11:24 (KJV)

Therefore I say unto you, What things soever ye desire, when ye pray, believe that ye receive them, and ye shall have them.

Rom 8:37 (ESV)

No, in all these things we are more than conquerors through him who loved us.

Let us pray: Father God, I come before You in the name of Jesus Christ, my personal Lord and Savior. First of all, I ask that You forgive me for my sins just as I forgive those who have done me wrong.

The Bible says in 1 John 1:9 that if I confess my sins, Jesus Christ is faithful and just to forgive me my sins and to cleanse me from all unrighteousness. Lord Jesus, You bore my sins in Your own body and by those wounds, I have been healed.

Right now, I take my authority as a believer, and I command this (Name the Problem) to leave my body in the mighty name of Jesus Christ. Satan, you are a defeated foe. I have the victory over all the works of the enemy because I am more than a conquer through Jesus who loved me and gave His life as a ransom for my sins. I command any unclean spirit inflicting me to leave my body right now, in the name of Jesus Christ. The Bible says that the name of Jesus is higher than every other name. Pain, sickness, disease and evil spirits have no power over me because I carry the name of Jesus.

The Bible says that when you stand praying, believe that you receive, and you shall have whatsoever for which you pray. Therefore, I believe by faith that I am healed. I receive my healing right now. The Word of God, the blood of Jesus, and the name Jesus Christ have healed me. I thank you, Heavenly Father, in the mighty name of Jesus Christ, for this wonderful miracle. You are Jehovah Rapha, The God who heals me. Amen.

Healing

1 Peter 2:24 (Jesus) who Himself bore our sins in His own body on the tree, that we, having died to sins, might live for righteousness - by whose stripes you were healed.

Say So: Father, I thank You that Jesus bore all of my sins and took stripes for all of my sicknesses. Since Jesus bore them for me, they have no place in me. Therefore, I receive Your free gift of grace and agree with Your Word by calling myself healed!

Psalm 34:19 Many are the afflictions of the righteous, but the LORD delivers him out of them all.

Galatians 3:13 Christ has redeemed us from the curse of the law, having become a curse for us...

Say So: Because of what Jesus did for me on the cross, I am delivered from the hold of sin and sickness and have the right to be free from every affliction that may come my way. Jesus paid the price for me and has redeemed me from the bondage of the curse. Therefore, I am saturated with His blessing of health and wholeness. It's mine now!

Romans 8:11 But if the Spirit of Him who raised Jesus from the dead dwells in you, He who raised Christ from the dead will also give life to your mortal (natural, earthly) bodies through His Spirit who dwells in you.

Say So: Father, because I have confessed Jesus as my Lord and Savior, your precious Holy Spirit is dwelling within me. Therefore, my present, natural body is continually being infused with resurrection power and life. The healing power of God is flowing through my body now, making my body healthy and strong.

Jeremiah 30:17 For I will restore health unto you, and I will heal you of your wounds, saith the Lord.

3 John 2 Beloved, I pray that you may prosper in all things and be in health, just as your soul prospers.

Say So: Father, I thank You for revealing Your will to me through Your Word. I thank You for the restoration of my health and for providing new life for me. I receive my health today and thank You for Your plan of prosperity, increase and wholeness in every area of my life. Therefore, I say: I am healed, and I am blessed!

Psalm 103:2-5 Bless the Lord, O my soul, and forget not all His benefits: Who forgives all your iniquities, who heals all your diseases, Who redeems your life from destruction, Who crowns you with lovingkindness and tender mercies, Who satisfies your mouth with good things, so that your youth is renewed like the eagle's.

Say So: Because my sins have been forgiven, health, healing and deliverance belong to me as a free gift from the Lord. Thank You, Lord, for encircling me daily with the many benefits of Your grace! My strength is renewed, and I am satisfied with the abundance of Your goodness daily!

John 8:36 Therefore if the Son makes you free, you shall be free indeed.

Romans 8:2 For the law of the Spirit of life in Christ Jesus has made me free from the law of sin and death.

Say So: Thank You, Jesus, I am indeed free from poverty, sickness and disease, for my life is governed by the law of the Spirit of life in Christ Jesus. Therefore, I am free from the law of sin, death, and the effects of death. I am increasing in health daily and call myself absolutely whole and made free!

Isaiah 54:17 No weapon formed against you shall prosper, and every tongue which rises against you in judgment you shall condemn.

This is the heritage of the servants of the Lord, and their righteousness is from Me, says the Lord.

Say So: I condemn the attack of sickness and disease and command it to fail and leave my body now! Sickness and disease do not belong to me. No weapon formed against me can or will prosper, for I am a redeemed child of God. Divine healing, health and wholeness are my covenant rights from the Lord!

Romans 8:16-17 The Spirit Himself bears witness with our spirit that we are children of God, and if children, then heirs - heirs of God and joint heirs with Christ...

Romans 8:32 He who did not spare His own Son, but delivered Him up for us all, how shall He not with Him also freely give us all things?

Say So: Thank You, Father, for Your love poured out to me. I am Your child now and a joint heir with Jesus. I receive Your free gift of healing and wholeness that You intend for me to have.

Healing belongs to me now and is my right as a child of God!

Psalm 107:20 He sent His word and healed them, and delivered them from their destructions.

Psalm 118:17 I shall not die, but live, and declare the works of the Lord.

Say So: Jesus is my Deliverer, Who was sent to bring about my healing and wholeness; spirit, soul and body. Therefore, I take hold of the finished work of the cross and command sickness and disease to leave my body now. According to the healing promises of the Word I say: I shall NOT die, but live, and declare the works of the Lord!!!

Mark 11:23-24 (Jesus said) For assuredly, I say to you, whoever says to this mountain, 'Be removed and be cast into the sea,' and does not doubt in his heart, but believes that those things he says will be done, he will have whatever he says. Therefore, I say to you, whatever things you ask when you pray, believe that you receive them, and you will have them.

Say So: I speak to all manner of sickness and disease and command you to leave my body now. You have no place here for I am a child of God. I make a demand on my body to come in line with the perfect will of God and produce a strong immune system and healthy environment that enforces life.

Psalm 91:9-13 Because you have made the Lord, who is my refuge, even the Most High, your dwelling place, no evil shall befall you, nor shall any plague come near your dwelling;

for He shall give His angels charge over you, to keep you in all your ways.

Say So: The Lord is my refuge and dwelling place; therefore, evil has no place in my life and any and all sickness or disease is off limits in my body. I belong to the Lord, and He is my life and has given His angels charge over me. Thank You, Lord, for Your great love for me - I am the healed and not the sick.

Proverbs 4:20-22 My son, give attention to My words; Incline your ear to My sayings. Do not let them depart from your eyes; keep them in the midst of your heart; for they are life to those who find them, and health (medicine) to all their flesh.2

John 6:63 ...The words that I speak to you are spirit, and they are life.

Say So: The Word of God is life and health to me, and it is medicine to all my flesh. As I stand in faith upon the Word, the Life of God is flowing through my body, infusing me with health. Everything that is not health producing must go from me now, in Jesus' Name.

Mothers & Daughters Anthology II

Hadassah's Crown Publishing, LLC

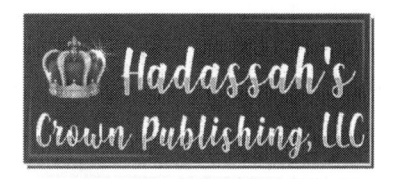

Made in the USA
Columbia, SC
07 July 2023